WHEN GOOD DOCTORS GET SUED

2nd EDITION

WHEN GOOD DOCTORS GET SUED

2nd EDITION

A PRACTICAL GUIDE FOR PHYSICIANS INVOLVED IN MALPRACTICE LAWSUITS

ANGELA M. DODGE, Ph.D.
with Steven F. Fitzer, J.D.

Updated Edition, February 2015

This book may not be reproduced in whole or in part, by electronic or any other means, which exist or may yet be developed, without permission of:

Dodge Publications
Olalla, WA

Contact: info@dodgepublications.com or adodge@dodgeconsulting.com

The material contained herein represents the opinions, views and professional experience of the authors, and should not be construed to be the views or opinions of the law firms or companies with whom the authors are associated or to whom the authors may have provided consulting services.

Nothing contained in this handbook is to be considered as the rendering of legal advice. Readers are responsible for obtaining such advice from their own legal counsel. This handbook and lists or question examples herein are intended for educational and informational purposes only. The primary author (Angela Dodge) is a litigation psychologist; she has no formal legal training, nor is she licensed to practice law in any state.

All rights reserved. No part of this publication may be reproduced, stored in a retrieval system, or transmitted in any form or by any means, electronic, mechanical, photocopying, recording or otherwise, without the prior written permission of the authors. For permission contact:

Dodge Publications
14591 Wiley Lane SE
Olalla, WA 98359
(253) 857-7716
info@dodgepublications.com or adodge@dodgeconsulting.com

For more information about publications and prices available through Dodge Publications, please visit the website at www.dodgepublications.com.

Copyright © 2015 by Dodge Consulting & Publications, LLP
Cover and text design by Kathy Campbell
Printed by Gorham Printing, Washington State
Printed in the United States of America

Updated Edition Printed February 2015
Second Printing April 2020

ISBN 978-0-9777511-1-2

DEDICATION

This updated handbook is dedicated
to the late Margaret Fahn,
an amazing woman who never forgot
the importance of taking care of others first

OTHER BOOKS AVAILABLE FROM DODGE CONSULTING & PUBLICATIONS LLP

Available at **www.dodgepublications.com**
or at **www.amazon.com**

The Better Witness Handbook:
A Guide for Testifying at a Deposition, Hearing, or Trial

by Angela M. Dodge, Ph.D. and John H. Ryan, Ph.D. (July 2013).

ISBN 978-0-9777511-9-8 (Print Edition $19.95)
Also available for Kindle

Preparing Witnesses to Give Effective Testimony:
The Attorney's Essential Guide

by Angela M. Dodge, Ph.D. and John H. Ryan, Ph.D. (April 2013).

ISBN 978-0-9777511-6-7 (Print Edition $24.95)
Also available for Kindle

Winning at Jury Selection:
A Handbook of Practical Jury-Focused Techniques & Strategies

by Angela M. Dodge, Ph.D. (July 2010).

ISBN 978-0-9777511-4-3 ($34.95)
Not currently available for Kindle

Opening Statements-Closing Arguments

by Ronald J. Matlon, Ph.D. (Second Edition, 2009).

ISBN 978-0-9777511-3-6 ($19.95)
Not currently available for Kindle

CONTENTS

1. **HOW THIS BOOK CAN HELP YOU; A WORD FROM THE AUTHORS** 1
   - What You Will Get for Your Investment 2
   - Who Should Read This Book 3
   - Notes to the Reader 4
   - An Additional Resource 4

2. **BASIC ANATOMY OF A MEDICAL MALPRACTICE LAWSUIT** 5
   - The Legal System as Foreign Turf 5
   - What is Medical Malpractice? 5
   - Proving Medical Negligence 8
   - When it is Not Medical Negligence 10
   - A Few Terms You Should Know 10
   - Basic Steps in a Medical Malpractice Lawsuit 13
   - You and Your Attorney 14
   - The Role of Medical Experts 15

3. **WHY GOOD DOCTORS GET SUED** 17
   - How Frequently Doctors Are Sued 18
   - Who is Most at Risk for a Malpractice Lawsuit? 18
   - The Good News 20
   - Why Patients Sue Their Medical Providers 21
   - Social Factors in Medical Negligence Lawsuits 22
   - Can Malpractice Lawsuits Be Avoided? 23

4. **COPING WITH THE EMOTIONAL TOLL OF BEING SUED** 25
   - The Personal Toll 26
   - Common Emotional Reactions 27
   - Mental Replays 29
   - The Importance of Your Attitude 29
   - Regaining Control 30
   - Using Positive Self-Talk and Positive Imagery 30
   - A Little Help from Family and Friends 32

5. **GIVING A GOOD DEPOSITION** 35
   - The Basics of a Deposition 37
   - What a Deposition is Not 37
   - Common Misconceptions 38

Unique Challenges That Doctors Face... 41
Plaintiff Attorney's Goals.. 42
Your Goals for the Deposition... 43
The Importance of Consistency 44
Logistics of a Deposition 45
What to Expect from Opposing Counsel 46
Basic Ground Rules 46
If Your Deposition is Video-Recorded.. 47
Attending Other Depositions.. 47
Some Legal Rules You Should Know About Depositions 48
Preparation for a Deposition is Critical.. 49
Insurers Recognize the Need For Preparation 50
Suggestions For a Pre-Deposition Trial Run.. 51

6. THE ART OF ACTIVE LISTENING... 53
What is Active Listening?.. 53
Barriers to Active Listening 54
The Consequences of Poor Listening... 54
Recognizing Patterns of Poor Listening.. 55
Overcoming Listening Barriers.. 57
Taking Time to Listen... 57
Diagnosing Questions: What to Listen For 58
Listening for "Mental Alarms" 62
Taking Listening Breaks.. 69
Getting Some Practice... 70

7. ANSWERING QUESTIONS EFFECTIVELY................................ 73
Common Pitfalls During Cross-Examination.. 73
Two Biggest Fears About Cross-Examination....................................... 74
Concerns About Memory 76
Sources of Information for Answering Questions.................................. 76
The Limits of Memory 79
Typical Areas of Questioning at a Deposition...................................... 79
Cardinal Rules to Follow in Answering Questions................................. 83
A Note on Medical Records 90

8. AVOIDING QUESTION TRAPS 93
Common Attorney Traps and How to Handle Them............................... 94
No One is Perfect 113
A Laundry List of Things to Avoid 113
Handling Difficult Situations.. 114
A Test of Your Diagnostic Skill... 116

9. WINNING DEFENSE STRATEGIES ... 121
Common Plaintiff Theories ... 121
Effective Responses to Plaintiff's Themes ... 127
Combating Plaintiff Theories Can Be Challenging ... 135

10. LITIGATION AND ELECTRONIC MEDICAL RECORDS (EMRs) ... 137
Changing Patient and Juror Expectations ... 137
Claims of Spoliation and the Dangers of Screen Shots and Pull Down Menus ... 138
Explaining Auto Populate Entries ... 139
Unrealistic Communication Expectations ... 139
Importance of Medical Records to Jurors ... 140

11. IF YOU GO TO TRIAL ... 143
What Happens at a Trial ... 143
How Trial Testimony Differs From Depositions ... 145
Answering Questions at Trial ... 146
The Importance of Pre-Trial Preparation ... 149
About the Jury ... 150
Be an Educator, Not a Defendant ... 151
Developing Rapport With Jurors ... 152
When Jurors Can Ask Questions ... 153
Hearing Expert Witness Testimony ... 154
Those Annoying Little Habits ... 155
Demeanor and Dress ... 156
When the Case Is Given to the Jury ... 157
Pre-Trial Jitters ... 158
Post-Trial Decompression ... 159

12. THE POCKET GUIDE ... 161
Things to Remember About Malpractice Lawsuits ... 161
Things to Remember About Emotional Reactions ... 162
Things to Remember About Depositions ... 162
Things to Remember About Your Goals at Deposition ... 163
Things to Remember About Listening ... 163
Things to Remember About Answering Questions ... 164
Things to Remember About Going to Trial ... 165

ABOUT THE AUTHORS ... 166
Angela Dodge, Ph.D. ... 166
Steven Fitzer, J.D. ... 167

ACKNOWLEDGMENTS

The information, ideas, strategies, and sample questions and answers in this book come from many years of experience in the area of medical malpractice litigation, and from exchanges with many people—extraordinary lawyers, their clients, other trial consultants, insurance representatives, colleagues, friends, and many good doctors. Thanks are owed to all of these people, and they will know who they are.

Heartfelt gratitude is owed to Bertha Fitzer, J.D. for her helpful comments on and thoughtful corrections to this updated volume, as well as her individual contribution (see Chapter 10). Her welcomed input improved this edition immeasurably. Special thanks are also extended to the president of Dodge Consulting & Publications, John Ryan, Ph.D., for his valued contributions to this edition.

We wish to extend our appreciation to the many colleagues, healthcare insurance representatives, and healthcare professionals who offered suggestions regarding needed updates and additions, and who supported our efforts to prepare this second edition.

1

HOW THIS BOOK CAN HELP YOU; A WORD FROM THE AUTHORS

"A physician into whose life litigation comes is like a patient with an acute, unpleasant, yet survivable disease."

—FROM *DOCTORS AND THE LAW* BY ZOBEL AND ROUS

Medical malpractice lawsuits are an increasingly frequent reality for any physician practicing medicine today. Regardless of specialty, location, years of practice, or pedigree of education, the chances are high that sometime during one's career, a physician will be summoned to defend her or his care and treatment of a patient. In doing so, most physicians will find the legal system idiosyncratic, contradictory, frustrating and intimidating. Filled with emotions that range from fear and disbelief to resentment and rage, few medical professionals will feel completely confident giving sworn testimony at their deposition or at trial, and even fewer will emerge from those situations feeling assured they have been effective truth-tellers.

Facing a lawsuit is a frightening and confusing event in anyone's life, but particularly so for those being accused of causing harm to patients they are pledged to help. Although many doctors have given testimony as a treating physician or as a medical expert, being a "defendant" in a malpractice lawsuit involving six- or seven-figure damages is a very different kettle of fish. Often professionally embarrassed, angered by accusations of incompetence or neglect, and fearful of repercussions, many medical professionals believe they have few places to turn to for the practical advice and support they need during litigation. More accustomed to providing help than seeking it, many defendant doctors mask their anxiety and simply don't ask.

Some of the anxiety surrounding a lawsuit comes from uncertainty and confusion about the process. Working with defendants, we have been asked everything from the appropriate color of clothing to wear at trial, to how to deal with aggressive cross-examination; from how long a deposition will last, to what happens if you are found "guilty." A frequent question is, "Are there any books or articles on what to expect and what is expected of me during the lawsuit?" Unfortunately, there were few practical resources. This guidebook, and its original predecessor, have helped to change that.

Just as a physician might treat an "acute, unpleasant yet survivable disease," we have attempted in this book to provide not painful remedies or quick cures, but effective ways to increase your sense of personal control, weather the process as comfortably as possible, and reduce somewhat the long-term negative after-effects of the ailment. The treatment may take time and attention, but it will help you not only to survive, but to become stronger.

WHAT YOU WILL GET FOR YOUR INVESTMENT

Because of their demanding schedules, few doctors have time for additional reading. For the busiest practitioners, we have summarized the most important information at the end of the book. These summaries are dubbed "The Pocket Guide." It is better to read only the pocket guide than nothing at all.

For those who take the time to read the text completely, your rewards will be substantial. They include the following benefits:

- Practical information in non-legalese language you can use immediately to reduce anxiety, form realistic expectations, and increase your personal feelings of control and self-confidence during litigation;

- Acquaintance with essential legal terms and an outline of the typical process followed in malpractice litigation;

- Understanding the goals and purposes of your testimony;

- Sensible advice for becoming a more accurate, careful, and believable truth-teller at a deposition or at trial;

- Many examples, exercises, and tips to improve listening skills, avoid lawyer traps, and handle difficult cross-examination questions;

- Information on dress and demeanor that are appropriate for deposition and for trial that will enhance your likeability and credibility; and

- Acknowledgment of the intense emotions you will experience at various stages of a lawsuit, along with strategies for coping with the inevitable strain caused by malpractice litigation.

This guidebook is not intended to replace thorough preparation by a defense attorney, but to enhance it. It's not meant as a game day "playbook," but as a prescription to help alleviate your anxiety and increase your ability to be an *effective and believable truth-teller* when giving testimony. Although we suggest various techniques for giving compelling and convincing answers to questions you may be asked at a deposition, arbitration, or trial, our focus is not on *what* to say, but rather on *how* to say it. With the advice of defense counsel, with practice and the application of the techniques provided in this guidebook, you can greatly improve your performance as a witness and substantially strengthen your case.

WHO SHOULD READ THIS BOOK

Although for brevity we refer to "defendant doctors" or "physicians," the information and suggestions we offer can help any medical professional who has been named as a defendant in a malpractice lawsuit, or who will be serving as a witness in such a lawsuit. These include nurses, physician assistants, midwives, therapists, podiatrists, chiropractors, dentists, and others with liability for patient care.

This guidebook is also recommended reading for spouses and partners of defendants. Most spouses are deeply concerned about a lawsuit and its effects on their partner. Discussing this guidebook with a spouse or partner will help him or her better understand the unique stresses of a medical negligence lawsuit, equip them to provide emotional support, and help everyone survive the most stressful periods of the litigation. Family members can also be recruited as coaches and a sounding board for some of the communication exercises suggested in the book. Spouses or partners are more able to provide support when they, too, understand the steps a defendant will be going through and what to expect at each phase of the lawsuit.

The book may also help expert medical witnesses, attorneys preparing witnesses, other trial consultants seeking additional knowledge on medical malpractice witness preparation, medical students needing well-rounded preparation for their careers, and law students. We hope that insurance claims representatives, risk managers, and others will find useful information in these chapters.

NOTES TO THE READER

Rather than using the cumbersome designation of "he or she" or "s/he" when referring to an attorney or a medical professional, we balanced the use of "she" and "he" throughout the book, recognizing that attorneys and medical care providers are represented by both genders.

Some terms are used interchangeably. The attorney representing the party who is bringing the lawsuit is most often referred to as the "plaintiff's attorney" or "opposing counsel." The attorney representing a healthcare defendant is referred to as "your attorney" or "defense counsel."

When a patient name is needed in an example or sample question-answer exchange, "John Doe" or "Jane Doe" is used. Any resemblance to a real Mr. or Ms. Doe is accidental.

Examples of specific question-and-answer exchanges may or may not have been taken from past cases that are now public record. Any similarity or resemblance to a pending case is accidental.

AN ADDITIONAL RESOURCE

Witnesses whose roles in a malpractice lawsuit lie outside the medical practice arena (e.g., administrators, risk managers, record-keeping staff, etc.), may find the authors' parallel publication, *The Better Witness Handbook* (ISBN 987-0-9777511-9-8), more appropriate.

2

BASIC ANATOMY OF A MEDICAL MALPRACTICE LAWSUIT

"Just because someone has been injured, it does not mean that someone (else) is at fault."

—FROM *THE EXPERT WITNESS HANDBOOK* BY POYNTER

THE LEGAL SYSTEM AS FOREIGN TURF

For most physicians the legal arena is a complex, adversarial, and intimidating system, as foreign to them as an operating room to an attorney. With its own language, rituals and rules, the legal process can mean confusion, anxiety and exasperation to any "outsider."

A medical professional entering the legal system experiences a unique form of mental stress. You are accustomed to people seeking treatment, advice and education. You are used to patients entrusting you, relying on your skills, depending on you to fix a problem. You are used to speaking your own language and using precise technologies and treatments. When you enter the legal system, that comfort zone disappears; instead, you face judges, attorneys and a complex web of unfamiliar rules and laws. Now *you* are the outsider, intelligent and educated but not in control. Add to this the challenges to your professional reputation, and the tension multiplies. Learning just the basics of malpractice lawsuits can help reduce that anxiety and enable you to feel a little more comfortable with the language that is used.

WHAT IS MEDICAL MALPRACTICE?

A malpractice lawsuit is a *civil* case brought to determine *negligence* (failure to meet the standard of care), *causation* (chain of events and consequences), and *damages* (money to be awarded to the plaintiff). "Guilt" is a legal term that applies in criminal cases only, not in civil lawsuits. In order for the defendant healthcare provider to be found liable for damages in a civil case, the jury must find the defendant negligent, *and* that the negligence was a "proximate" (i.e., directly related) cause of the plaintiff's injury. Only then can damages be determined.

Malpractice lawsuits may name one or more doctors, healthcare facilities, medical personnel such as nurses and physician assistants, a medical practice group, laboratory, pharmaceutical company, or any entity believed to have contributed to the alleged negligence.

The burden of proof that a medical provider or healthcare facility was negligent rests with the plaintiff. Even though defendants are not required to prove their innocence in medical malpractice lawsuits, it is surprising how many physicians, facing a legal claim, act defensively and insist that they be "proven innocent."

Negligence and Standard of Care

While state law typically determines how negligence is defined, and thus differs slightly from state to state, "standard of care" is the yardstick for measuring malpractice. It's not a measure of *optimal* care, or even of what a medical expert thinks should have been done. The issue is whether any reasonably prudent medical professional would have done what the medical provider (e.g., doctor, nurse, etc.) in question did, based on available information and resources.

The standard of care is not the same as the quality of care, which encompasses the adequacy of the total care patients receive from healthcare professionals. And unless the standard of care is violated, mistakes and complications, whether expected or unexpected, do not necessarily constitute malpractice.

The standard of care is perhaps best understood as "ordinary care," which requires the healthcare provider to follow standards that do not vary unreasonably from the general practices of similarly trained providers with similar resources, practicing under similar circumstances. However, negligence cannot be excused just because other physicians practice similarly. Actual practice must meet a reasonable, prudent standard of care.

Standards defining "acceptable practice" or "ordinary care" can come from medical experts, medical literature, practice guidelines, hospital policies and procedures, state and federal regulations, and other relevant sources. The standard of care in a particular community is usually established at trial by medical expert testimony. In some states, this testimony must be established before a patient or a patient's family can initiate a lawsuit.

Contrary to popular opinion, most people who sue for malpractice are not fakers or malingerers, but have suffered a real injury or loss. The issue in a malpractice case is whether the injury was the result of negligence, or of misfortune. In some cases, patients themselves have contributed to the injury or loss, either because of their own negligence or a failure to follow advice; in other cases, it is a sad fact that something bad has happened to a blameless person.

Negligence From a Juror's Perspective

A major challenge for most defense attorneys in medical malpractice cases is the lack of understanding, or misunderstanding, among jurors regarding the concept of *standard of care*. When asked in pre-trial research or post-verdict interviews how they would define the concept, jurors have offered a surprising variety of definitions, including:

- "Negligence means the doctor neglected to do something he should have." (Note: This is the most common definition.)

- "A doctor doing what is best for the patient, at the time, based on his or her training."

- "Doing what he or she is supposed to do."

- "Doing what he or she has been taught in medical training to do."

- "The very best care for the patient that is available at the time."

- "Following the accepted procedures of the hospital."

- "The doctor has an obligation to do his or her best with the patient's best interests in mind. If that has been done, the standard of care has been met."

- "Due care and caution. Putting the patient, not yourself or your needs, first."

- "Following the generally accepted procedures and doing nothing to harm the patient. If the patient is harmed, it is likely the standard of care was violated."

- "Giving the patient the best care possible."
- "If the doctor didn't do everything to eliminate risks of the treatment or procedure, it is negligence."
- "If the doctor could have or should have done more, and did not, it is negligence."
- "When errors are made and the patient is hurt, the standard has been violated."

Even though jurors are provided with the legal definition of standard of care before they begin deliberations, these responses show there can be considerable differences in how jurors conceive the standard of care. This can directly affect how they decide medical negligence cases. Appreciating the way in which jurors evaluate violations of the standard of care can help the defense develop more effective trial strategies. It can also help defendant healthcare defendants to understand how answers to questions regarding standard of care might impact jurors' perceptions.

Who Will Be Involved

Defense costs are typically paid by the medical malpractice insurer, based on the coverage. An experienced claims representative from your insurance carrier will be actively involved in your case. The representative hires an attorney who specializes in medical malpractice defense to represent you, and closely monitors the lawsuit. The defense team consists of you, the insurance representative and your attorney. Your attorney will likely hire medical experts to testify on your behalf, and a trial consultant or communications specialist may be employed to help you prepare for deposition and/or trial.

PROVING MEDICAL NEGLIGENCE

The standard of proof required in medical negligence cases applies in most civil cases: *a preponderance of the evidence*. It's not necessary to prove negligence "beyond a reasonable doubt," as in criminal prosecutions. The plaintiff's attorney must prove a *causal link* between the physician's actions or lack of action and damage to the patient.

For a claim of medical negligence to be proved, the plaintiff's attorney must demonstrate one of several possibilities related to the actions or inactions of the defendant. These include:

1. The doctor or medical provider *did not perform up to the standard of care* expected of his specialty. The standard is defined as that of a "reasonably competent physician" in that specialty, not the most experienced or least qualified. A general practitioner, for example, must be judged by the standards of her specialty peers, not of thoracic surgeons. However, if a general practitioner attempted a specialist's task, the standards of that specialty would apply. The important criterion is whether the diagnosis and treatment were reasonable.

2. The doctor *failed to inform* the patient of the risks, likely benefits and possible alternatives to the treatment so that the patient could make an informed decision about the treatment. Failure to obtain informed consent is often a claim in medical malpractice lawsuits, even though a treatment consent form may have been signed by the patient.

3. A *delay or error in diagnosis*, resulting in further injury or premature death. Less common claims are: failure or delay in performing a procedure, failure to order a requested test, failure or delay in referring a patient to a specialist, or an error in a pathology laboratory analysis. Certain diagnostic procedures and medications can also result in claims.

4. The doctor *breached a contractual duty* to provide reasonable medical care. In rare cases, the plaintiff may file claims under state or federal laws regarding consumer protection or discrimination.

Most lawsuits focus on breaches of the standard of care and lack of informed consent. Complaints typically ask for both economic damages (specific financial losses such as hospital or doctor bills, funeral expenses, lost wages, nursing care costs, home modifications, etc.) and non-economic damages (subjective non-monetary losses such as pain and suffering, loss of enjoyment of life, loss of chance for survival, loss of function, loss of support). The patient's spouse and minor children can also claim loss of companionship due to the medical negligence, and request additional damages.

A plaintiff may seek *punitive* damages against a defendant who engaged in reckless or malicious conduct. In some states, punitive damages are disallowed; in others, a "cap" or maximum amount of damages is specified by law.

In states that apply statutes regarding a marital community (i.e., community property), a spouse may also be named as a defendant. This is a legal technicality. In community property states, a spouse has a legal right to half of the marital assets, and also faces half the liabilities. The naming of a spouse in a malpractice lawsuit does not mean the spouse is considered negligent, merely 50% liable for any damages that might be awarded to the plaintiff. Whether or not a named defendant, a spouse may be urged by counsel to attend the trial for other reasons, such as to provide emotional support.

WHEN IT IS NOT MEDICAL NEGLIGENCE

No cure is guaranteed in medicine, nor is a medical complication alone evidence of negligence. Complications are part of the risk in any medical treatment. The choosing of one method of treatment over another, when several exist, is not malpractice. Physicians are not held to the highest standard of care in their specialty, and cannot be proven negligent if they followed accepted practices in the community. Physicians cannot be held liable for "honest mistakes" if they have taken a proper history, done a thorough examination of the patient, used appropriate diagnostic tests, and shown reasonable judgment. Special allowances also apply when a physician acts in an emergency. The fact that a patient has a bad outcome does not constitute malpractice. The ultimate determination of negligence, however, resides in the court system, not the medical arena.

A FEW TERMS YOU SHOULD KNOW

Knowing some common legal terms will make you feel less like an outsider. Following is a basic lexicon that will get you through most of the legal events and settings you will encounter.

TERM	DEFINITION OR MEANING
Plaintiff(s)	The person(s) bringing the lawsuit against you. It may be the patient, the patient's family, or a legal guardian.
Defendant(s)	The party or parties against whom the lawsuit is brought. There may be many defendants, and defendants can include hospitals, the physician's practice group, clinics or labs, and anyone who was involved in the plaintiff's care. In community property states, the spouse may also be named.
Discovery	A pre-trial phase of a lawsuit when both sides must disclose relevant facts, documents, and other evidence. The objectives are to locate evidence, preserve testimony, narrow issues, and avoid surprises.
Direct examination	Initial questioning of a witness at trial by the attorney who called the witness. It is usually followed by cross-examination and possibly redirect examination.
Cross-examination	Questioning of a witness at trial by a lawyer other than the one who called the witness about matters he testified to in direct examination.
Redirect examination	Questioning of a witness by the attorney who originally called the witness, after she has been cross-examined.
Adverse witness	Whenever counsel for either side calls an opposing party to the stand, the witness is "adverse." For example, if the plaintiff's attorney calls you to the stand while presenting her case, you are considered adverse, or "against" the plaintiff. This strategy is sometimes used by plaintiff's counsel.

TERM	DEFINITION OR MEANING
Testimony	Any questioning done under oath that is recorded or transcribed, whether at deposition or trial.
Motion	An oral or written request made to the judge by an attorney regarding a legal rule or order.
Objection	Made whenever either attorney asserts that a witness, line of questioning, or piece of evidence is improper and should not be continued, then asks the judge to decide. If there's an objection during a deposition, you may be required to answer the question anyway, and it will be ruled on later, at trial.
Complaint	The first pleading of the plaintiff(s), setting out their facts and allegations.
Interrogatories	A pre-trial discovery tool in which written questions are submitted to the opposing side and to which a written reply, under oath, must be made. Interrogatories are often the first step in establishing facts known by defendants.
Deposition	A pre-trial discovery tool in which a witness is cross-examined under oath by opposing counsel, all of which is transcribed. A deposition may be taken of any witness, and it may be video recorded.
Reasonable medical certainty	The legal measure of probability meaning "more likely than not." It can also mean a "preponderance of the evidence (51% or more)" or that the amount of evidence is slightly more weighted on one side than the other. It does *not* mean absolute certainty.
Standard of care	Standards of behavior on which the theory of negligence is based. It requires the "actor" to do what a "reasonable person of ordinary prudence" would do in the actor's place. In medicine, the standard of care is that of a "reasonably competent physician in that specialty."

BASIC STEPS IN A MEDICAL MALPRACTICE LAWSUIT

Although no one will expect you to become a legal eagle, you will be a more effective witness at your deposition or at trial if you understand the basic legal process in which you are expected to perform. With a rudimentary understanding of the steps and rules that apply in malpractice litigation, you will be more confident, better able to cooperate with the defense strategy, and less likely to be tripped up by the opposing attorney.

Every malpractice lawsuit is unique, but most cases proceed through the same basic steps. Typically, it takes from two to five years to get through the complete process. Some lawsuits are even longer. Of course, a case can be dismissed or settled before it goes to trial—and many are. If the lawsuit is not settled, you will be involved in all the following steps:

1. A *Complaint* is filed by the plaintiff(s), the person(s) bringing the lawsuit. You are served with the legal notification, usually at your office. This is often, but not always, your first awareness of a claim.

2. Your insurance company hires a *defense attorney*. He contacts you and then answers the complaint, denying some or all of the claims. The insurers may also retain expert consultants to review the case and advise them about the lawsuit's strengths and weaknesses.

3. The *discovery phase* begins. The aim is to avoid presentation of unexpected testimony in the courtroom. During this phase, the attorneys for all parties usually exchange relevant documents such as hospital records, clinic charts, lab test results and radiographic studies. You will be asked to complete a set of interrogatories, or written questions about your education and medical experience, and the facts you know about the case. Written replies are made under oath, with the assistance of your attorney. During the discovery phase, your deposition and the deposition of the plaintiff(s) are taken. Other witnesses may or may not be deposed. In depositions, witnesses are questioned by opposing counsel. The deposition is important: some medical malpractice attorneys consider it the most important element of your defense. Several chapters of this guide are devoted to helping healthcare defendants prepare for a deposition.

4. *Settlement* may be negotiated between you, your attorney, the plaintiff, the plaintiff's attorney and the insurer. If no settlement is reached before trial, your trial date is set by the court. Some defendants view settlement

as "caving in" or admitting negligence; others realize it may be the least risky and most cost-effective resolution.

5. *Trial by jury* is held (see note below). The plaintiff's case is presented first, then your case. You will be one of several witnesses testifying on your behalf. The plaintiff's attorney will have one or more expert witnesses testify that your care below acceptable standards. Your attorney may or may not present expert witnesses to testify on your behalf. Admissible evidence and testimony are presented to the jury. The length of the trial varies, depending upon the complexity of the case. As a defendant, you will attend the entire trial with your attorney.

6. A *verdict* is delivered. The jury decides if the evidence proves you were negligent, and if so, if your negligence caused injury or death. If this is the case, the jury also decides how much money is to be awarded the plaintiff.

7. Either side may *appeal* an adverse verdict, but appeals must be based on questions of law, not merely an unsatisfactory verdict. Appeals are heard by a panel of judges and no new evidence is taken.

YOU AND YOUR ATTORNEY

Although you have the right to consult a personal attorney at your own expense, your malpractice insurance carrier will select and pay the attorney who defends you. Successful malpractice defense attorneys are known to insurers, and you should trust their judgment to select a capable and experienced advocate to defend your case.

A close, professional relationship with your attorney is essential. Just as patients must trust a physician they know little about, you must trust your attorney implicitly. Relate to your attorney just as you want patients to relate to you. Be informative, honest, optimistic, and receptive to professional advice. It is important to talk with your attorney about any previous legal experiences, and to avoid enthusiastic agreement with Shakespeare's often-quoted words: "The first thing we do, let's kill all the lawyers." Making your attorney an adversary will only add to your challenges. Instead, devote your energies to educating and assisting him.

> **Note:** In rare instances, the right to a jury trial may be waived, in which case a verdict is rendered by a judge. Also, the parties may agree to have the case decided outside the court system by a retired judge or by an arbitrator.

Once your attorney has been engaged, let her handle all communications. Contact her about legal documents or other communications you receive. Make no personal contact with the plaintiff or anyone involved with the plaintiff. It is unethical for the plaintiff's attorney to communicate with you once you are represented by counsel. Notify your attorney immediately if that happens. Direct all requests from plaintiff's counsel to your attorney. If you are contacted by a plaintiff's attorney *before* you become a defendant (and thus do not have legal counsel), notify your insurance carrier immediately.

THE ROLE OF MEDICAL EXPERTS

With limited exceptions, medical malpractice lawsuits rely on experts. Experts are hired to define the applicable standards of medical care, testify whether you deviated from those standards, and provide opinions regarding the causal link between the alleged negligence and the plaintiff's injuries. Expert medical witnesses typically review medical records and other materials to make their determinations.

The job of experts hired by plaintiff attorneys is essentially to persuade the jury that whatever your level of competence is, in *this case* you acted negligently and your negligence was a direct cause of injury to the patient. Your attorney typically identifies medical experts whose reviews show support for the care or treatment you gave. The defense expert's job is to dispute the plaintiff expert's medical opinions and support your performance, arguing that it met the standard of care. Experienced malpractice defense attorneys keep a roster of credible experts to call on. Trust that your attorney has weighed many factors (expertise, reputation, availability, juror appeal) when selecting experts. However, your suggestions are likely to be welcomed.

Your reactions to the reports of plaintiff's medical experts are fairly predictable. You will reject them, argue against their conclusions, question the expert's qualifications, or feel guilty because an expert with prestigious credentials disagrees with your care. You will develop defensive arguments. These are common and normal reactions to criticism. After your blood pressure returns to normal, identify for your attorney the expert opinions and conclusions you feel can be challenged.

Despite your reactions, the reality is that even the most perfect work is subject to criticism. It is good to express your anger and resentment, or mere dismay, about what an expert has concluded. However, such expressions should be shared with your attorney in private. Remember that even the best doctors can disagree about the best ways to treat a medical problem.

There are instances of medical negligence for which expert testimony is not needed in order to establish negligence. Leaving a sponge in a patient's body or operating on the wrong knee are examples of obvious negligence. In such cases, your defense team may admit liability and agree to pay reasonable damages, but even this is not always the case.

Understanding the anatomy of a malpractice lawsuit reduces some unknowns. But the nagging question remains: "Why me?" The answers you find in the next chapter may surprise you.

3
WHY GOOD DOCTORS GET SUED

*"When it comes to malpractice lawsuits,
nearly everyone is eligible."*

—UNKNOWN SOURCE

If you are a doctor or any other medical provider who is being sued for medical negligence by a patient or a patient's family, you're not alone. Thousands of doctors, nurses, physician assistants, and the facilities in which they work are sued each year, in every state, in every specialty, for nearly every reason imaginable. Since 1985, according to the American Medical Association (AMA), the overall claims rate has declined, but how analysts define "claim" and what data are included are variable factors. However, one can say that if you are practicing traditional medicine today, the odds are fairly high that you will be named in a lawsuit sometime during your career. The odds may be even greater in high-risk specialties. Many doctors now admit they have unhappily accepted the reality of a potential lawsuit at any time—from the first day to the last day of one's professional practice.

Malpractice Lawsuits Are Not New

Although the incidence rates have fluctuated, malpractice lawsuits are hardly new. The first recorded lawsuit for medical negligence in the United States was filed in 1794, and between 1835 and 1865 the courts were inundated with malpractice cases. When data on claims frequency became more available in the 1950s, both the number and severity of claims were relatively stable. In the late 1960s and early 1970s, the frequency of claims began to increase at unprecedented rates, as did the dollar amounts awarded to plaintiffs. In the next sections we share what is known about how often doctors are sued, who is most likely to face a malpractice lawsuit during a medical career, and what the cost of malpractice litigation can be.

HOW FREQUENTLY DOCTORS ARE SUED

There have been few nationwide studies calculating the proportion of doctors who are sued in a given year, the proportion who have lost a lawsuit and made an indemnity payment, and the size of payments made. However, a fairly recent (2011) study published in the *New England Journal of Medicine* (NEJM) has shed some reliable light on these questions. Overall, the study reported that one in 14 doctors (7%) faces a malpractice lawsuit every year. Over their careers, most physicians and nearly every surgeon will face at least one malpractice claim during their work life.

A survey released in 2010 by the AMA has also provided data on the incidence of malpractice claims. The analysis found that more than 60% of physicians have been sued by age 55. Male doctors are twice as likely as female physicians to get sued during their career, and more doctors in solo and specialty practices are sued than those in multispecialty practices.

Bases for Malpractice Lawsuits

The majority of malpractice cases involve diagnostic errors or delayed diagnoses that cause harm. A 2012 analysis by Diedrich Healthcare, a liability insurer for medical professionals, indicated that the highest proportion of legal allegations (33%) are diagnosis related, 24% are surgery related, and 18% are treatment related. The remaining 25% were associated with obstetrics, medications, monitoring, or anesthesia. These percentages did not vary by much in their 2013 analysis.

Among cases involving treatment errors, the most claims are made against family practitioners, followed by specialists in internal medicine. Emergency room physicians and cardiologists are also high on the frequency list.

WHO IS MOST AT RISK FOR A MALPRACTICE LAWSUIT?

What is the riskiest specialty for lawsuits? There is substantial variation in the likelihood of a physician in a given specialty being sued, and in the size of monetary compensation across specialties The NEJM study reported that 75% of physicians practicing in *low-risk* specialties will be sued by the time they reach age 65, and 19% will have paid damages to a plaintiff.

Physicians in *high-risk* specialties such as surgery and emergency medicine are even more likely to be involved in malpractice litigation: 99% will have been sued by age 65, and 71% will have paid out monetary compensation. It is generally believed that physicians who specialize in obstetrics and/or gynecology are also frequent targets, often owing to child birth injuries or infant deaths.

What are the high and low risk specialties? According to the NEJM study, physicians with the highest risk of being sued were neurosurgeons and thoracic-cardiovascular surgeons (annual risk of about 19%). General surgeons had a slightly lower risk (annual risk of 15%), while pediatricians and psychiatrists had the lowest rates (annual risk of about 3%).

Physicians sued for malpractice are often assumed to be less competent than those never sued. Research has failed to support this opinion. A 1999 study of over 3,500 family physicians in Florida found just the opposite to be true—the frequency of malpractice claims was related to *greater* medical knowledge, not less. A Harvard Medical Practice Study in 1991 found that physicians who were negligent were unlikely to be sued, and physicians who were sued were unlikely to have been negligent. The most important variable appears to be the doctor-patient relationship: many patients are simply reluctant to sue a family doctor or a physician with whom they have a good relationship and a history of good care. However, don't assume that just because you have a strong, long-term relationship with a patient, and may perhaps even be continuing to provide care, that you are immune from being sued by that person. It may not be your patient who is actually the motivating force behind a lawsuit.

The Direct Costs of Malpractice Lawsuits

How much is actually paid out in malpractice lawsuits won by plaintiffs? Even though we hear about multi-million-dollar awards, such verdicts are uncommon, and awards that exceed common policy limits (i.e., $1 million) are actually rare. The average medical malpractice payout is much less.

According to the National Practitioner Data Bank, a total of $3.6 billion was paid out to plaintiffs in 2012, with an average payout of $300,000 per case. During that year, five states represented nearly half (48%) of the payouts—Florida, New Jersey, California, Pennsylvania, and New York. The total payout in 2013 increased by 5%, for a total of $3.7 billion. Male patients made up 43% of all malpractice payouts in 2012; females accounted for 57% of payments.

The bulk of insurance payouts appear to be from settlements rather than from bench or jury trials. In 2012, only 5% of payments to plaintiffs resulted from judgments (i.e., trials). In 2013 the percentage of payout amounts that were determined by judgment was only 3%.

The Indirect Costs of Malpractice Lawsuits

Physicians can insure themselves against lawsuit payments through malpractice insurance, but they cannot insure against the indirect costs of litigation such as the significant emotional costs. Time losses, stress, added work, professional embarrassment, and reputational damage are real costs that cannot be accurately measured. However, as any physician who has faced a malpractice claim knows, these costs can be staggering.

Analyzing data from over 40,000 physicians covered by a nationwide insurer, a study by RAND Corporation found that the average physician spends almost 11% of an assumed forty-year career with an unresolved, open malpractice claim. The amount of time required to resolve such claims can be distressing for both patients and doctors. Coping with the emotional toll of malpractice claims is an important issue addressed more comprehensively in Chapter 4.

THE GOOD NEWS

Although the data on malpractice lawsuits and payouts might appear somewhat alarming, there is some good news, too. According to data assembled by Physician Insurers Association of America (PIAA), most malpractice lawsuits never make it to the courtroom. The study reported that 65% of malpractice claims filed were dropped, dismissed, or withdrawn. About one in four claims were settled out of court, and about 5% were decided by alternative dispute mediation. Of the 5% that went to trial, defendant doctors won a defense verdict in 90% of the cases.

Why do so few cases go to trial? Whenever possible, insurers try to settle out of court to avoid the stress and astonishing expense of litigating a case to a jury verdict. The relative strength of the plaintiff and the defense cases, as well as the risk of a high damage award, are also considered. For some plaintiffs, settlement for an amount less than desired is preferable to a legal process that could take years.

Why do most cases tried by a jury end in a defense verdict? Some people believe it is because doctors are held in high regard and thought to be incapable of causing harm. In reality, many factors come into play. These include the strength of evidence, the competence of the attorneys, the communication skill and credibility of the defendant doctor(s), the believability of medical expert witnesses and the venue where the case is decided.

While defense attorneys are skilled at predicting probable verdicts, the reality is that such predictions are only educated guesses. Seasoned attorneys know that a perfectly defensible case can be lost at trial, just as a case that appears risky may result in a favorable verdict. If you're named in a suit, you should assume the case will go all the way to a jury, and prepare to cooperate with your defense team to that end. If the case is dismissed or settled out of court, so much the better.

WHY PATIENTS SUE THEIR MEDICAL PROVIDERS

Surprisingly, a relatively small percent of those injured by a physician's negligence ever file a claim or seek compensation. Given the expense and other difficulties involved in bringing a lawsuit to court, it is doubtful that most claims are filed on a greedy whim, and very few frivolous lawsuits are accepted by plaintiff attorneys who earn nothing if their clients lose at trial.

The most obvious reason for a suit is that a patient, or a patient's family, experienced an unfortunate result and believes it was due to substandard medical care or ill-informed decision-making. Many people seek to assign blame or retribution for a poor medical outcome, or an unexpected or unexplained result. Often the patient or family is angry, or grieving, or anxious about coping with a disability and related financial burdens. Others seek social justice, or public acknowledgment that they have been injured. Some want to punish a particular physician or hospital, or the medical community in general, for an inaccurate prediction or unfortunate outcome. Some hope that money will help compensate psychologically for their loss. Others may view an unfortunate outcome as an opportunity to achieve compensation for other social or economic disadvantages they have suffered.

But of all the reasons good doctors get sued, the most prevalent is money. And while it is very personal to the defendant being sued, for many plaintiffs a lawsuit is simply a means to obtain money for past bills and anticipated future losses. They may justify their decision by the belief that the money is being paid, after all, by an insurance company, not by their hometown doctor. Such is more likely when there is little rapport between patient and physician.

There are people—some of whom may be jurors—who view malpractice lawsuits as a way to "police" a profession they feel is reluctant to punish their own. And some view lawsuits as the only recourse for those who feel they have been damaged by a doctor. A few of the more cynical want to "send a message" to the medical community that it must do a better job.

Whatever the plaintiff's motivation, a physician can take comfort in knowing that few people sue because they intend to ruin a doctor's reputation or his financial security, close down a clinic, or prevent a needed medical procedure from being performed on others. Most plaintiffs would admit their motive is simply compensation for losses, not profit. Keep in mind that a lawsuit can carry a high psychological toll for both sides.

SOCIAL FACTORS IN MEDICAL NEGLIGENCE LAWSUITS

Recent increases in the number of malpractice lawsuits are also considered the result of social forces that have changed the traditional doctor-patient relationship. These include:

1. Patient dissatisfaction with "managed care." A great many people feel medical care has deteriorated under managed care systems. They complain that it is easier for patients to "fall through the cracks," or to be denied tests and referrals because these reduce insurance company profits.

2. Increased consumer awareness. Consumers are demanding more from the services they receive. Increased Internet access to medical information (such as WebMD), and a growing trend to take more responsibility for one's own health, means more savvy patients who are better informed about procedures and treatments, and less tolerant of inferior treatment outcomes. As self-advocates, they may distrust physicians' motives and the policies of medical insurance companies in general, viewing them as adversarial to the consumer.

3. Minimal up-front cost to the patient to file a lawsuit. Plaintiff attorneys often work for a percentage of money awarded, called a contingency fee, and are paid only if the case is won.

4. Rapid innovations in medical technology. These advances have created unrealistically high expectations by the public, while sometimes carrying increased risks.

5. Increased expectations that given sophisticated testing and advanced procedures, physicians should be able to avoid complications and ensure positive outcomes.
6. The human predisposition to blame others for bad outcomes or unfulfilled expectations.

CAN MALPRACTICE LAWSUITS BE AVOIDED?

What can be concluded from the studies that have been done on malpractice claims? The most common denominator for all targets of malpractice lawsuits is simply the doctor being in practice. An old adage is that medical professionals fall into two groups: those who have made a mistake and those who are going to make one. The same patient who expresses gratitude and relief one day may sue the next day. What you see as a minor flaw in an otherwise excellent outcome may be the subject of a serious medical claim for a dissatisfied patient who anticipated a perfect outcome. In fact, many a physician has been heard to remark after being served with a malpractice complaint, "But I saved her life!"

Regardless of your specialty area, where you practice, how long you have practiced, your level of expertise, or the types of patients under your care—you are at risk. While the probability of being sued varies from location to location and specialty to specialty, there is simply no guarantee that you can avoid a lawsuit. However, there are some ways to help reduce your risk.

Factors That May Reduce Risk

Increasingly, risk managers see the *doctor-patient relationship* as the chief preventive factor in malpractice claims. The idea of forming a "partnership" in which both the patient and the physician collaborate in health recovery is gaining importance. The assumption is that taking responsibility for one's own recovery can moderate the tendency to blame the physician when something goes wrong. Paying attention to the nature of the relationship in which feelings of helplessness, dependency, and disappointment are minimized may be helpful in nipping a potential lawsuit in the bud.

A second major factor is *informed consent*. It's difficult for anyone to lodge a complaint about an unfortunate outcome when the risks, benefits and alternatives to a treatment or procedure have been thoroughly discussed with the patient, and the patient has agreed in writing to assume those risks. Many defense attorneys would agree, in fact, that the stronger the informed consent process, the stronger your defense is likely to be. This does not mean that all possible risks and potential complications must be outlined. The standard of care requires only that the most common risks and complications be discussed. Many patients believe, however, that the most life-threatening potential risks warrant discussion, regardless of incidence rates. Clear, reality-based discussions with the patient and the patient's spouse or family, and *thorough documentation* of the discussion, can be a significant deterrent to negligence claims.

A third factor is how *you react* once an error or unexpected result occurs. Although it would be inappropriate and perhaps legally unwise to acknowledge blame when an unfortunate outcome has occurred, it is important for you to recognize the patient's feelings. "I feel bad that this happened."—"I am sorry you had this outcome."— "I know you are feeling frightened and disappointed."—"I know you are going through a lot of pain." These are all compassionate statements that reflect your concern. As part of the partnership you have established, your patient needs to hear your expressions of sympathy. Don't confuse these expressions of concern, however, with admissions that you or the hospital acted negligently, and are to be held legally responsible.

It is not uncommon for plaintiffs to admit in a deposition that at least part of the motivation to file a legal claim stemmed from the hospital's or the physician's inability or unwillingness to explain what happened. Lacking information, and experiencing what may appear to be a physician's avoidance of the patient and/or family members, some plaintiffs conclude a lawsuit is the only way to learn "what really happened" or "what went wrong, and why." The time when the patient or family may need the physician most is when the outcome is unexpected, unfortunate, or the result of a known but unfortunate complication.

4

COPING WITH THE EMOTIONAL TOLL OF BEING SUED

"Anxiety is what kills."

—CHIEF JUSTICE HOLMES

Few legal proceedings ignite emotion in a doctor more fully than a claim of medical negligence. The accusation of causing harm or even the death of the patient can be devastating. Reactions of medical providers to malpractice lawsuits represent the entire spectrum of emotion, from annoying distraction to shock, disbelief and anger, bitter resentment, or a career-shattering blow. Doctors who are sued for malpractice feel betrayed, hurt, threatened, vulnerable, frightened, embarrassed, very often depressed, and certainly anxious. Not only do reactions vary, but they often shift over time as issues are clarified. A feeling of stark terror one month may be replaced by cautious optimism the next. Indifference in the early stages of the lawsuit may evolve into extreme stress as the trial nears. How you might react depends on your personality, personal and professional support network, litigation experience, and most importantly, your resilience and ability to cope.

Lawsuits are serious events and can have long-reaching impact. Some physicians who have been sued, regardless of the outcome, have become more risk-averse and their practices have become more limited or cautious. Others consider a medical malpractice lawsuit a "life-changing event." Embittered by being sued by a patient and fearful of other lawsuits, some doctors begin to question whether they want to remain in medicine. A small percentage have left their practices and sought careers in less litigious professions such as teaching or research. Other doctors, determined not to let litigation influence their practice, have simply grown a thicker skin.

THE PERSONAL TOLL

Regardless of the effect of a lawsuit on one's medical practice, the personal toll is often substantial. The stress of an unfortunate medical result, followed by a frightening legal entanglement is an emotional one-two punch. A malpractice lawsuit can rekindle painful memories of an unhappy outcome for a patient, even though you may have done all that you could. Knowledge that a patient is permanently affected by a bad outcome can be a disturbing thought that lingers in your memory. Sometimes, a death has occurred—parents have lost an infant, a young husband has lost his wife, or children have lost a father—and grief affects everyone involved in the patient's care. The resurgence of these memories can be an additional source of stress during litigation.

Doctors being sued often experience a loss of confidence and self-esteem. For some defendants, the mere fact that a patient had an unsuccessful outcome compels them to assume blame. A lawsuit can put great strain on other aspects of doctors' lives, including work and family relationships. They are often professionally embarrassed; a few are personally devastated.

Doctors who have made personal and financial sacrifices to practice in small cities and rural areas are particularly sensitive to the effects of a lawsuit. In these situations, being sued for malpractice can be both an embarrassment and a source of deep resentment.

Lawsuits take a long time to resolve. Just when you have begun to put the painful event in the back of your mind, some case-related activity will arise: a deposition to be taken, additional records to be provided, an expert's opinion to review. The lawsuit never really disappears. Like the *Poltergeist* ghost, just when you have forgotten about it, "IT'S BACK!" The cyclical nature of litigation stress can be more damaging than the consistent pressures that doctors face daily.

Even though malpractice insurance will cover the cost of your defense, you will undoubtedly experience some financial losses. Time necessary to prepare for a deposition, attend trial, read legal documents, review medical records, and meet with your attorney is time away from your work. This can impact income and benefits such as vacation time.

COMMON EMOTIONAL REACTIONS

Although each physician's reaction to being sued is unique, certain emotions seem commonly experienced. Following are the reactions frequently observed or reported among doctors who are being sued, and some of the underlying thoughts and emotions. Your particular emotional reactions may vary somewhat from these patterns, but don't be surprised if you experience any of these strong sentiments at various stages of the litigation process. They are typical and expected; the sooner you recognize and get past them, the better able you will be to cooperate in your defense.

Emotion	Underlying Thoughts
Annoyance	You are hard-working and your schedule is already overflowing. Now you must meet with attorneys, review files, answer interrogatories, attend depositions—all at the expense of your other patients and your family. You resent the time that is required to prepare your case.
Diminished confidence	Allegations of wrongdoing shake your faith in yourself and in your competence; your self-assurance drops.
Self-criticism	Feeling you have fallen short of the expectation of perfection, you begin doubting your competence, your skills, and your judgment. You begin to wonder if you belong in medicine.
Over-analysis	Using a "retrospect-o-scope" you begin pouring over every aspect of your treatment and the patient's record, looking for the detail that will exonerate you. You obsess about details of your treatment. You spend long hours researching the literature for supportive material.
Resentment and feelings of betrayal	You feel betrayed by the patient for whom you went the extra mile, or by the patient whose life you probably saved—the ungrateful patient who has now betrayed you by filing a lawsuit. You are enraged at the term "negligence" because you know you did everything possible. You become testy, sullen or on edge.

Emotion	Underlying Thoughts
Anger	Your resentment turns into anger—at the patient, then at *all* patients, the hospital, the court system, *their* attorney, *your* attorney, family members and on and on. Your animosity toward and distrust of attorneys grows exponentially. Your family life may begin to suffer and this creates even more resentment.
Fear and anxiety	Fears begin to occupy your mind: fear of the financial consequences if a jury awards millions of dollars, fear of being reported to the National Practitioner Data Bank, fear of loss of referrals or a drop in patients and income, fear of becoming uninsurable or having to pay even higher premiums, fear of losing control, and fear that your reputation is irreparably damaged. Anxiety control may be attempted through drugs or alcohol.
Worry over loss of control	You begin to feel anxious over the loss of control and authority you are accustomed to exercising. You may fear or distrust the entire legal system, about which your knowledge is limited and over which you have little control. You worry how you will ever find time for the necessary preparation when your schedule is already overcrowded. You dread the idea of non-physicians (jurors) judging your performance, and wonder how you can explain to lay people the complexities of the medicine involved.
Disbelief or denial	You refuse to acknowledge that a patient would ever sue you, insist that the lawsuit is frivolous, deny any wrong-doing, and become indignant when asked to participate in your defense. You begin to think the lawsuit has been drummed up by an aggressive plaintiff's attorney.

While there are great differences in reactions, and in the intensity of various reactions, the key is to avoid letting emotions interfere with your ability to cooperate effectively in your defense. It is also important to openly express your feelings to your attorney. She needs to know.

MENTAL REPLAYS

Some defendant doctors also engage in "if-only" thinking. Despite confidence that you did everything right and that no other physician could have achieved a better outcome, the very presence of the lawsuit generates an obsession with mental replays. "If-only-I-had…." or "If-only-I-had-not…" These scenarios that attempt to rewrite past decisions and actions can easily leave you filled with self-doubt. When you become obsessed with past events and repeated playbacks, your chances of becoming depressed, embittered, and emotionally drained will escalate.

How can you combat these mental replays? Look back over your medical career. Which patients had the best recovery in the shortest time? Those who looked back or those who looked toward the future? Those who dwelled on the painful and frightening events of their illness or injury, or those who focused on regaining strength and returning to a normal life? There is nothing to be gained from morbid replay. There is much to be gained from reassuring yourself you did everything you could. Experiencing strong emotional reactions is both expected and common. Getting beyond them in order to remain focused on patient care is essential.

THE IMPORTANCE OF YOUR ATTITUDE

One of the best ways to cope is to take the advice you give your own patients: Be optimistic. Success is the result of a team effort involving your defense attorney, the insurer, witnesses who testify on your behalf and yourself. However, the most important member of the defense team is *you*. Your attitude plays a big role. If you are pessimistic, uncooperative, and unable to trust legal professionals, your outcome is at risk. Just as you tell your patients, it's important to focus on what you can do to help. Keep your expectations and spirits high and look toward a good outcome.

Just as there are no guarantees in medicine, there is no guarantee you will emerge from a malpractice lawsuit completely exonerated. But that reality must not diminish the commitment of everyone, including you, to doing their part well. Never let it slip from your mind that as a physician, you are an intelligent and educated professional who is no stranger to pressure and high expectations. You are accustomed to exercising sound judgment and making rational decisions. Don't lose sight of those strengths.

REGAINING CONTROL

A major source of anxiety for defendants is the fear of losing control. Reading this book will help alleviate some of that. You will also feel more in control if you have concrete and practical ideas about what you can do to assist in your defense. Here are some suggested activities. Share these thoughts with your attorney.

1. **Identify your vulnerabilities.** In what areas of your care exist the likelihood of the greatest professional disagreements? What do you think could have or should have been done differently? How sound are your reasons for the judgments or decisions you made? How do your decisions stack up against possible alternatives?

2. **Review your medical records** for any problems in documentation. You should make no changes to the written record except by dictation for clarification, which must be dated at the time of the review.

3. **Develop your own version** of a timeline that clarifies what you did and when you did it, starting with your first contact with the patient. Where does "your story" begin?

4. **Start a notebook** that includes a) questions and matters you wish to discuss with your attorney, b) your recollection of events at issue in the case, c) journal or textbook references pertinent to the case and d) copies of all court documents you have received.

5. **Start a personal journal** in which you record your feelings and concerns as the lawsuit progresses. Journaling is an effective stress management and self-exploration tool, and it is also a good problem-solving mechanism.

The key point is that any action is preferable to brooding about the doom and gloom of a lawsuit. But obsessive preoccupation with your defense is not healthy either. Remain focused on what you do best—patient care—and let your attorney focus on what he does best—defending you.

USING POSITIVE SELF-TALK AND POSITIVE IMAGERY

In their timeless book on rational psychotherapy, Ellis and Harper assert, "You feel as you think." This idea, inherent in the doctrine of positive self-talk, simply means that the sentences we create and repeat to ourselves are powerful determinants of our emotions, self-esteem and general well-being. Your anxiety level is escalated by internal, often unconscious repetition of negative thoughts. Self-criticism such as, "I'm such an idiot. I should have known better."—"I was just too stupid to see what was developing."—"Any fool could have diagnosed that problem."—"The attorney is going to know I messed up."—only serves to depress you. Replacing these sentences with more positive thoughts helps control anxiety and improve your attitude.

Whenever you catch yourself becoming depressed and anxious about the lawsuit, pay attention to the negative self-talk you are generating. Unplug that tape and insert a different one—one filled with positive affirmations and optimistic self-talk. Make a conscious effort to begin repeating to yourself some the following thoughts:

"I am a competent, confident, and caring physician."

"My conduct was not negligent, no matter what someone else says."

"The patient's complaints about my conduct have not been proven."

"I did everything in my power to help the patient."

"I'm well-prepared for my deposition."

"I am in control of myself and my testimony."

"I will be thoughtful and careful. That's the kind of person I am."

"I have done nothing wrong and have nothing to feel guilty about."

"This is a challenging time and my strength will get me through it."

"I have helped thousands of patients and have saved many lives."

Do this while driving to work, taking a shower, walking to a meeting, getting your lunch, or scrubbing for surgery. Start producing positive words, phrases, sentences, and beliefs in your mind. The only criteria are that the thoughts must be deliberate, repetitive, forceful and confidence-building. Repeat these positive affirmations for at least five minutes before entering your deposition or taking the witness stand at trial.

Visualize what you *want* to happen in a realistic and positive way. See a picture of yourself being congratulated by your attorney for a good job after the deposition. Imagine the feeling of elation you will have at the end of your deposition or your trial knowing you have conducted yourself competently and professionally. Another anxiety-reducer is to picture the lawsuit in the context of your larger "life picture." Image yourself sitting in the courtroom, put a frame around that picture, and then place that frame in the context of your entire life— growing up, going to school, getting your medical degree, becoming a licensed physician, establishing your practice, getting married, buying a home, having a family. In larger context, the lawsuit's importance will be more realistic. Keep reminding yourself that "this, too, shall pass."

A LITTLE HELP FROM FAMILY AND FRIENDS

Often doctors feel there is no one they can really talk to about the lawsuit and how it is affecting them. They've been told by their attorneys *not* to talk to anyone about the case (see Note below). This can cause a doctor to feel isolated and alienated from peers and friends. Add this to the stress of the lawsuit, and the result is often "compassion fatigue." There is little left for your patients when your emotional resources are drained.

Some physicians do not tell their spouses or partners about the impending lawsuit until it is absolutely necessary, hoping it will settle quickly, eliminating the need to expose the family to the inevitable worry and fear. Some doctors are hesitant to tell their children. Perhaps they don't want loved ones to see that their parent is vulnerable, or they fear the loss of regard of family members. In reality, telling your spouse and children (if they are old enough to understand) about your predicament has several advantages. Telling children what is happening, and why, can head off unrealistic fears of Mom or Dad going to jail or losing the family home. Informing your spouse opens the door to discussing what can be expected, how your partner can best support you, how you will deal with rumors or newspaper stories. It is a good idea to alert your family about what to expect and how they should interpret your behavior.

> **Note:** State law determines the scope of privileged communications, the most common of which is the attorney-client privilege. Your attorney can explain the scope of privileged communications (e.g., spouse, pastor, counselor, etc.), and you should have this discussion early on to avoid waiving your privileges.

It is not unusual for spouses to feel the need to "share the burden" of the lawsuit. While you may believe the best place for your spouse or partner is at home keeping things as normal as possible, your mate may feel differently. In addition to providing emotional support, your mate may want to: a) be a "communication coach" in practicing some of the exercises in this book or the suggestions made by your attorney, b) attend your deposition or be with you at trial, c) discuss how to minimize other demands on your schedule to allow you the time to prepare, or d) gather information on the issues involved in the case. Regardless of the role you and your partner find is appropriate, the important thing is that you talk about the lawsuit, how it is affecting you, what is likely to happen over time, and what can be expected.

One thing to avoid is isolation. Finding a source of support—a spouse, partner, pastor, parent, adult child, psychologist, close friend—is an important first step when you become a defendant. You need not discuss the case with your confidant—merely your feelings about being sued. If necessary, you should never hesitate to seek professional help from a psychologist or psychiatrist. This does not imply weakness. Acknowledging your fears and concerns is healthy. A trial consultant or litigation psychologist experienced in litigation stress management may be a particularly helpful resource.

Your attorney may offer to put you in touch with other physicians who have gone through the lawsuit process. If offered, take advantage of this. "Veterans" of malpractice lawsuits are often willing to share their experiences. Ask your attorney about the availability of such options.

A word of caution: You may be asked at your deposition with whom you have spoken about the case. Anyone you name (unless they fall into the category of privileged communication) is a candidate to be deposed by opposing counsel. Ask your attorney with whom you may discuss the impact of the lawsuit to make certain you understand the extent of privileged communications. Remember that talking about the emotional impact of a lawsuit is different from talking to someone about the specific issues.

Lastly, do what you can to regain a sense of control by managing your expectations and reactions. Begin viewing yourself as a member of a team—you, your attorney, the insurance company, your spouse and family, a trial consultant—all of whom are dedicated to helping you win your case. You are not alone. And never forget that there is life after a lawsuit.

5
GIVING A GOOD DEPOSITION

*"The will to succeed is important,
but what's more important
is the will to prepare"*

—RETIRED COACH BOBBY KNIGHT

Whether the malpractice lawsuit against you is resolved before trial or proceeds to a jury verdict, chances are you will be required at some point during the discovery phase to give an oral deposition. A deposition is essentially the examination of a witness, under oath, in question and answer format, during the pre-trial discovery phase. It is a vital step in your defense, and the importance of giving a credible and effective deposition should never be underestimated. Short of a jury trial, it is also the most stressful litigation step you will experience.

Unfortunately, doctors often do not perform well in their depositions or on the witness stand, largely because of: 1) naive conceptions about the purposes of the deposition, 2) misconceptions about their role, or 3) inadequate preparation on how to listen to and answer questions effectively. The following statements reflect the variety of experiences and reactions defendant doctors have expressed when not adequately prepared for their depositions.

WHAT DOCTORS HAVE SAID ABOUT THEIR DEPOSITIONS

"I was nervous about the aggressiveness of the other party's attorney. I didn't expect that."

"I have painful memories about not being able to say what I wanted to say."

"I forgot I was the defendant and started acting like the expert. This got me in trouble."

"I kept trying to give good answers to bad questions."

"I thought I did okay. It wasn't as bad as I expected."

"It was much worse than I expected. I wasn't prepared for some of the questions [he] asked and I got confused."

"I was so nervous I forgot everything. I probably looked like an idiot."

"I just said 'I don't know' a lot. That's what I thought I was supposed to do."

"I was asked questions in areas I didn't think were relevant to the lawsuit. I was surprised [opposing counsel] could do that, but I learned that at a deposition, nearly everything is fair game."

"I couldn't sleep the night before the deposition. And I never have trouble sleeping!"

"I just didn't want to be manipulated, but I found out [attorneys] have ways of asking questions to get you to say what they want to hear."

"I was so afraid [the attorney] would get me to say something wrong."

"When I finally read my deposition, I realized I had talked way too much and said some things that made me look bad. But it was too late."

Doctors' beliefs about depositions are often formed through limited experience, such as testifying on behalf of a patient, or rendering a medical expert opinion. When you become a defendant in a malpractice case, however, the rules of the game are more complex and the stakes are much higher. Approaching your deposition with erroneous beliefs can hurt your performance and possibly your case. As a first step you need a clear understanding of what a deposition is, and what it is not, as well as its purposes and goals, from both sides of the table.

THE BASICS OF A DEPOSITION

Because it is "discovery," the range and scope of what may be asked in a deposition is somewhat wider than what is permissible at trial. For example you may be asked about previous lawsuits, practice partner arrangements, social relationships with other defendants, or how many times you attempted but failed certification exams. Some of these inquiries may not be allowed at trial, but they may be asked at a deposition. Your attorney will intervene if a question falls outside the range of reasonable discovery, but you should expect to be required to answer questions put to you, even if you think they are unrelated to the case facts.

The product of a deposition is a typed transcript and/or video recording of everything that was said—every question asked and every answer you gave. The transcript is evidence, and as such, can be introduced and used against you at trial. The laws on the nature and extent of discovery through oral depositions depend on certain general rules, as well as those unique to a particular state or county. Regardless of the specifics, however, most plaintiff attorneys share common goals for deposing defendant doctors.

Many defendants leave the deposition feeling as though they have been competing at a disadvantage in an elaborate word game. They had expected a straightforward question-and-answer session in which they would tell their side of the story, the attorney would understand their actions, and rational thinking would prevail. Few have such satisfaction. Many defendants can expect to depart the deposition feeling disappointed, disheartened and uncertain about their effectiveness.

WHAT A DEPOSITION IS NOT

While it's important to know what a deposition is, it is equally critical to understand what it is *not*. First, a deposition is *not* the place for you to educate the plaintiff's attorney about anatomy, surgical techniques, or treatment procedures. It is opposing counsel's job to educate herself. Whatever she wants to know about the medicine at issue in the case, she must ask.

At your deposition, you are to volunteer nothing. Giving information beyond the scope of the question is the single most common error made by witnesses.

Secondly, a deposition is not a conversation. It's not a friendly give-and-take between two people. During normal conversations, we embellish, hide a lack of memory, gossip, ramble, speak without thinking clearly, tell little white lies and sometimes get distracted. In a deposition, these conversational habits can cause serious problems. Communicating effectively in a question-answer format is difficult. Preparation for your deposition will focus largely on the language, techniques, and self-discipline you will need to adapt to this unnatural situation. At a deposition, none of the informal rules of social conversation apply. A deposition is unique, and the rules for depositions are fairly rigid. Many of your social skills—charm, persuasiveness, ingratiation, personal warmth—are largely wasted in a deposition. Such skills may have an impact only on a jury.

Lastly, a deposition is *not* an HBO Friday night boxing event. At all times, be alert and cautious, but be careful not to cross the line into the arena of being resistant, uncooperative, or verbally combative. Do not try to match wits with or "one up" the attorney. No matter how intelligent you are, or how verbally skilled, you will lose. Remember that you are on legal, not medical turf, and the playing field is rarely even. You will do best by remaining composed and focused at all times, and by leaving the boxing gloves at home.

COMMON MISCONCEPTIONS

Most witnesses, including physicians, enter a deposition as adversaries, with misconceptions about appropriate strategies. Overcoming these beliefs and being more realistic increases your effectiveness. Let's look at these misconceptions and contrast them with reality.

Misconception	Reality
If I "tell my story" during the deposition, the plaintiff's attorney will realize his client has a weak case and drop the suit.	The deposition is *not* the place to tell your story. It might reveal sources or facts not previously known to the plaintiff and actually strengthen his case. It's not possible to "win" a deposition by convincing counsel that you are right and they are wrong.
I should confine my answers to "yes," "no," or "I don't know."	These responses are appropriate if they're true and complete answers. If not, they may misrepresent your testimony and are not appropriate. How can you appear knowledgeable and competent at trial if your deposition is full of "I don't know" answers.
I will be asked questions only about the issues specific to the case—the what, when, and why of my role in the treatment of the patient.	The deposition is opposing counsel's "fishing expedition" during which you may be asked questions that do not sound relevant. If the questions are too far afield, your attorney will object. But expect questioning to cover a wide scope.
If I am allowed to explain, I can influence the opposing attorney's thinking about various issues in the case.	Opposing counsel's thinking will not be influenced in this way. "Explaining" may reveal new sources of information for the opposition.
I need to tell my story because if the case is settled, the truth will never be known.	The time to tell your story is in court. If the case does not go to trial, be relieved. You will have to accept the absence of public exoneration.

Misconception	Reality
If opposing counsel gets tough with me, I'll get tough right back.	You must maintain your composure and control your emotions. If you are easily baited, opposing counsel will win and you will lose. Never get angry or argumentative; emotion interferes with logic and focus.
I can outsmart the attorney. She probably knows little about medicine.	Attempts to outsmart an attorney are rarely successful. In fact, they usually backfire. Most plaintiff attorneys will have a good grasp of the medical issues, and will know what to ask you. Remember, lawsuits are their area of expertise, not yours.
I'm angry and feel inconvenienced by all of this. Opposing counsel needs to know this so he will speed things along.	Opposing counsel may be delighted to know you are feeling angry, since it will interfere with your good listening.
Opposing counsel is in control and the only moves I can make are defensive.	As the witness, you are largely in control. You control the pace, the clarity with which questions must put to you, the precision of your answers, your emotional state, your demeanor, and your energy level. That is considerable control!
A deposition is like a chess game and I can out-maneuver opposing counsel by anticipating his moves.	Depositions are not about strategy or anticipating tactics. They are simply about answering one question at a time. Do not attempt to figure out opposing counsel's strategy. This will only distract your attention.

A few defendants have been given faulty advice by colleagues or friends who have themselves been deposed. Each malpractice case is different. What was effective in one person's case may not be effective, or may even be harmful in yours. The best rule is to follow the advice of your attorney, insurance representatives and the attorney's consultants. Although your attorney should be the final authority, your own common sense is also a good ally.

UNIQUE CHALLENGES THAT DOCTORS FACE

In addition to common misconceptions, doctors face several unique challenges when giving a deposition. First, your entire philosophy and training has been to help the patient, but now your goal is to defeat him. This is against your professional commitment. It's not how you are seen by others, and how you view yourself. Your natural tendency in a deposition is to feel responsible, remorseful, and off-balance. To compensate, you try to help plaintiff's counsel by volunteering information and answering poorly worded questions. You are also accustomed to educating patients and their families—part of your role as a "helping" professional. At deposition, explanations and education for the benefit of opposing counsel are discouraged. Yet it will be difficult for you to control your habit of encouraging understanding, particularly when the questions relate to the medicine involved—your arena of expertise.

Doctors are accustomed to being in control—of their practice, an operating theater, and in some instances, life or death. In the legal system, you will not feel in control because you are not the expert. Feeling out of control is anxiety-provoking for many people, particularly for medical professionals.

Lastly, the listening skills developed by physicians may work against you. While you're listening to patients describe their symptoms, your mind is considering needed tests, formulating diagnoses, reviewing treatment options and observing non-verbal behavior. You're listening to segments of information, rather than to each word. This type of listening makes you effective as a doctor—but vulnerable as a witness. (More on this in the next chapter.)

At this point you may feel you've got two strikes against you: your training as a helper is at odds with your best interests, and the opposition is poised to take advantage of your instinct to help. But understanding your role and the objectives of opposing counsel will help you suppress these natural tendencies.

PLAINTIFF ATTORNEY'S GOALS

Although their questioning routines and styles may differ, all plaintiff attorneys have specific goals in taking the deposition of a physician. It will help you to have a clear and realistic understanding of opposing counsel's intent. All of the following objectives play a role in plaintiff's deposition questioning.

- Gather information from you. What are your credentials? What do you know about the issues? What did you do or not do, and why? What is your version of the events in question? What records exist? Are there sources of information not yet discovered?

- Evaluate you personally. How credible and confident do you appear? How good is your memory? Which questions produce strong reactions or anxiety in you? Do you have any "hot buttons?" How will you appear to a jury? How easily are you manipulated? Are you a good listener? Are you personable?

- Clarify legal issues. What information, if any, is not relevant and should be excluded at trial? Is negligence being admitted?

- Discover inconsistencies in testimony that can be used at trial to discredit you. Will you say something different at trial than in the deposition? Do your answers at the deposition contradict previous assertions? Does your memory of events differ from what others have testified, or from the medical records?

- If there are multiple defendants, can you be enticed into pointing fingers at fellow defendants? Will you throw another defendant "under the bus" in an effort to minimize your own culpability?

- Validate plaintiff "themes" that may be used to influence how jurors view the evidence. Is patient care subordinate to profit? Is there a pattern of negligence? Was the plaintiff treated differently? Were the caregivers inexperienced in this treatment? Was patient care poorly managed? Was communication lacking between medical providers?

- Create a permanent record of your testimony that will be studied carefully and may be used at a later time to impeach your credibility by identifying inaccuracies or inconsistencies.

Don't Help Opposing Counsel Achieve His Goals

Knowing opposing counsel's goals will make you feel more comfortable and aware, but don't let this tempt you into trying counter-measures or playing games. Be equally aware of any tendencies you have to try too hard, resist too vigorously, or bait opponents into I-can-outsmart-you contests. Remember that being prepared gives you an advantage, but no matter how much you know, opposing counsel will always know more about the law than you do. Your best tactic is to keep your objectives in mind at all times and focus on the questions put to you. That's the winning strategy.

YOUR GOALS FOR THE DEPOSITION

While plaintiff's attorney will have specific objectives in mind when conducting a deposition, you are not obligated to help him achieve those goals. On the contrary, your focus should be on what you want to achieve.

Many doctors hold erroneous beliefs about their own objectives in a deposition. They may believe a key challenge is to answer the questions with "yes," "no," or "I don't know." Some see the deposition as a chance to tell the entire story, regardless of what opposing counsel wants to know. For others, it is an arena for debating medical judgment or venting anger. None of these goals are on target and none will strengthen your case.

What, then, is the best advice? Your goals for the deposition are simple and straightforward. Apply these as rigorously as possible.

- *Always* tell the truth. There should be no discrepancies between your deposition and trial testimony. You can't be tricked or embarrassed if you are consistently honest.

- Learn and use techniques in this guidebook for listening carefully to every question and for avoiding question pitfalls.

- Stay on an even keel. Exercise control regardless of opposing counsel's demeanor. Leave your temper at home. Look as though you are eager to tell the truth. With this in mind you will appear (and feel) more relaxed and confident.

- Prepare well. Review the relevant records, review with your attorney any questions you can expect, and get into good mental condition. Practice your communication skills with your attorney and, if appropriate, a trial consultant.

- Be precise, careful, succinct and consistent.

You may leave your deposition feeling frustrated because you were unable to tell your side of the story, or because not all the facts were revealed. You may be disappointed that the "right" questions were never asked, or that opposing counsel did not appear to understand the case. If you have done a good job of confining your answers to only those questions asked, frustration will be an expected outcome. Remember that your story will be told in its entirety at trial (if it ever comes to that), in front of the people who will decide the outcome—the jurors.

THE IMPORTANCE OF CONSISTENCY

Consistency between your deposition testimony and what you say at trial merits emphasis. Any statement you make at your deposition can be used to impeach your testimony later. Opposing counsel can point out any inconsistencies in your deposition to encourage the jury to disbelieve you. A sample of this strategy:

> *"Now, Dr. Smith, remember when I took your deposition on July 3 of 2012 and you swore to tell the truth, just as you did in court today? And you recall when I asked you [quote from deposition transcript] and you answered [quote from transcript]? That's different from what you told the jury today, isn't it? So let me ask you, Dr. Smith, which is the truth? Were you lying then or are you lying now?"*

Such confrontations not only sting badly, but they can destroy your credibility. If staged at the beginning of your cross-examination, your confidence may be so shattered you become ineffective as a witness for the remainder of your examination.

LOGISTICS OF A DEPOSITION

Understanding the simple mechanics of what will happen at your deposition helps you avoid feeling intimidated. Anyone who is a party in the case, and his attorney, may attend your deposition. Your attorney attends the deposition with you. Expect the plaintiff(s), the plaintiff's attorney(s), and a court stenographer to be present. In some cases, a claims representative from your insurance company may attend.

It's not recommended that your spouse attend unless you're certain his or her presence will help your demeanor. In community property states, where spouses are named defendants in lawsuits, there is a legitimate reason for a spouse to be present. Ordinarily, their presence at the deposition is not required, and may actually be a distraction to you.

The length of a deposition varies, depending upon your role in the case and the breadth of facts known to you, as well as the style of opposing counsel. The treating physician's deposition is likely to require more time, for example, than that of someone who was only peripherally involved in a plaintiff's care. A long-winded attorney may keep you at a deposition longer than one who is time efficient. Depositions can be as short as an hour, and as long as several days. A typical time is several hours.

Depositions are usually taken in an attorney's office. It may be more informal than a courtroom, but the same rules apply. You should not mistake this informality as an invitation for casual conversation in which you reply to questions "off the top of your head." Deposition answers must be limited to those based on medical certainty, not medical guesses. Any statement you make can be introduced as evidence, and your deposition testimony cannot be changed. Remember that what is said at a deposition can be used again months or even years later.

After the deposing attorney has completed her questioning, your attorney may question you. This is rare, and such questions are typically limited to clarifying your opinions or correcting any misleading statements you made. Because the deposition is a discovery vehicle for the plaintiff, your attorney will limit his questions to avoid volunteering additional information. Expect your attorney to question you thoroughly under direct examination at trial, but not at the deposition. Although also rare, you may be questioned briefly by a co-defendant's attorney.

WHAT TO EXPECT FROM OPPOSING COUNSEL

Every attorney has his or her own style in conducting depositions. In some cases, your attorney will have had previous experience with opposing counsel, and may be able to tell you what to expect. Styles vary—from low key and friendly-appearing to aggressive, fast-paced and intimidating. Expect the worst style and be pleasantly surprised if it's milder. However, keep in mind that a friendly demeanor can be a tactic used consciously to induce you to reciprocate and trigger any tendency you may have to please others and be helpful.

The style of the attorney may be different between deposition and trial. At the deposition, the attorney may ask questions in a loud, accusatory manner in order to intimidate you. The same attorney in court may be calm and quite pleasant because jurors are now present. The contrast may surprise you!

The attorney conducting your deposition may not be the same attorney who questions you in court. You may be deposed by another member of the plaintiff attorney's law firm. This could be part of opposing counsel's strategy to assess your reaction to different styles of questioning, or to throw you off balance at trial. Keep in mind that your focus is on the *content of* questions, not on the style of the questioning attorney.

BASIC GROUND RULES

During your deposition, you will be sworn to tell the truth, and the questioning must comply with certain rules. Your attorney may object to a particular question, just as he or she might in a courtroom, but you may still be required to answer. The admissibility in court of the question and your answer will be determined later by the presiding judge.

Don't be fooled by opposing counsel's attempts to create a casual atmosphere. Act at all times as if you were being cross-examined in a courtroom, especially if the deposition is being videotaped.

Doctors often assume that since no jury is present, they need not worry about nervous habits, demeanor, dress, or pace. Not so! The plaintiff's attorney is evaluating your communication style and your demeanor, important factors in gauging your "jury appeal." Act and appear as though a jury is present.

Except when an attorney requests to go "off the record" and during breaks, the transcriber is recording every word spoken. A typed copy of the deposition is prepared and distributed to each of the attorneys and to you. You can then correct errors in transcription or slips of the tongue, but you cannot alter the substance of an answer. Refrain from talking with anyone at your deposition except your attorney or insurance representative. Comments made "off the record" but overheard by opposing counsel, or social conversation with the opposing party, can be brought into the deposition. The lawyers can engage in witty banter or sarcastic statements, but you should remain professional and circumspect in everything you say.

Bring nothing to the deposition except what your attorney tells you. You will induce cardiac arrest in your attorney by showing up at the deposition with an armful of research studies you determined would be instructive for opposing counsel.

IF YOUR DEPOSITION IS VIDEO-RECORDED

Many states allow the depositions of key witnesses to be video recorded. The reasons vary, but they may include the need to preserve the testimony of a witness who may be unavailable by the time of trial, or to put additional pressure on the witness. Specific questions and answers from your deposition may be shown to jurors at trial. Ask your attorney if opposing counsel has requested that your deposition be video recorded.

A camera may add to your anxiety, but you will adapt to it. Maintain eye contact with the questioning attorney, as it would likely be quite uncomfortable to answer to a camera. Be careful about looking at your own attorney before giving an answer. This could send the non-verbal message that you are seeking signals about what to say.

On camera, your demeanor and composure will be very important, as will your physical appearance. Professional dress will enhance the impression others form of you. If your deposition is to be video recorded, dress as you would if you were appearing at trial. Be certain to control any nervous mannerisms, as they are also being preserved.

ATTENDING OTHER DEPOSITIONS

As a defendant, you have the right to be at all depositions. Attending the deposition of the plaintiff's key medical expert (if taken) may assure that his opinions are fair and not exaggerated. You may also help your attorney by suggesting questions or explaining a complicated medical issue raised by the expert. In states where depositions of experts are not allowed, you may be asked to read and comment on any written reports prepared by experts.

Just as the plaintiff is allowed to attend your deposition as an observer, you may be present at his or hers. Your attendance at the plaintiff's deposition may actually be helpful. In your presence, the plaintiff may be reluctant to distort, exaggerate or falsify the facts. The plaintiff's testimony may refresh memories, suggest possible defense arguments, or stimulate a re-examination of the case's strengths and weaknesses. If you can't attend the deposition, you may be asked to read and comment on the transcript of the plaintiff's deposition or the deposition of a plaintiff's expert.

SOME LEGAL RULES YOU SHOULD KNOW ABOUT DEPOSITIONS

Just as there are guidelines and procedures governing medicine, so are there rules and practices governing a deposition. Your familiarity with these basic rules will help you avoid misunderstandings and possible blunders during the deposition.

Privileged Information and Conversations
Ask your attorney to clarify with whom privileged communications are protected from discovery by plaintiff's counsel. Opposing counsel cannot ask you about conversations you had with your attorney, with paid consultants in the presence of your attorney, or with those parties who hold a protected relationship with you (e.g., a clergyman, priest, counselor, public officer, etc.). This falls under privilege rules. She can ask if you met with your attorney, but that's about all. Results of any peer review process usually are also confidential. If you are uncertain about whether a question invades these privileges, remain silent and let your attorney respond. Your attorney will advise you on how to deal with questions regarding your preparation for the deposition. A typical response is that you met with your attorney to review issues and discuss possible areas of questioning. Any further disclosure is unnecessary.

Documents and Exhibits
You have a right to see any material from which opposing counsel might quote. Simply say, "I'd like to see what you are quoting from." You are allowed (and should take) the time to read it carefully.

Breaks and Side Consultations with Your Attorney

Although you may not take a break with a question pending, breaks are allowed and encouraged. If your energy is fading, if you lose your concentration or your temper, you may request a short recess. Breaks can't be used as a stall tactic to avoid certain lines of questioning. Avoid over-using your right to a recess, as frequent consultations with your attorney may make you appear fearful, incompetent, or manipulative. You don't want a judge or jury to learn that during your deposition you were excessively "coached" by your attorney during numerous breaks.

Understanding Questions Put to You

You have a right to understand every question, and you need not, and should not, answer a question whose meaning is not clear. It's not wise to assume that every question posed by an attorney is clear and well-articulated. Don't be hesitant to ask for clarification. Opposing counsel will initially instruct you that if you do not understand a question, you should say so. By abiding by this rule, you preclude later requests to alter an answer because you misunderstood the question.

PREPARATION FOR A DEPOSITION IS CRITICAL

No one can be told how to be an effective witness. "Just do as I say" rarely works to produce a precise and succinct witness. Solid preparation requires discussion with your attorney, practice, feedback, and adjustments to listening and communication habits. It is unlawful for anyone to induce you to testify falsely or to influence your statements. However, it is completely proper, ethical, and strongly encouraged for you to meet with your attorney to discuss the events at issue in the case, outline possible areas of questioning, review documents, and practice relevant question-answer scenarios. The plaintiff will be doing exactly the same.

Preparation vs. Coaching

Good preparation is not "coaching." Coaching is telling someone what to say, or how to hide the truth. Witness coaching is unethical and may be illegal. Preparation, on the other hand, is a responsible act by your attorney. Preparation improves *how* you express your statements to ensure they are truthful, thoughtful and accurate. Good preparation will not, and should not totally eliminate anxiousness. Social scientists have shown that some nervousness is actually helpful in sustaining energy and motivation.

Adequate preparation is important because it can help you and your attorney identify habits that may need to be overcome to increase your effectiveness at deposition or trial. Once recognized, you will immediately see ways to improve your abilities. The result is a careful and precise deposition—one that holds no "surprise testimony" for your attorney. A pre-deposition preparation session, also referred to as a "mock deposition," should be held as close in time as possible to the deposition to ensure information is fresh in your mind.

Pre-trial preparation is also strongly encouraged. In some cases, attorneys have taken healthcare defendants to the courthouse to familiarize them with the courtroom and help de-sensitize them to inevitable anxiety. It also helps to know in advance where to park, which entrance to use, and what security screening is required.

Preparation significantly reduces fear of the unknown and builds confidence. Just as heart surgery patients benefit from a tour of the operating room and the chance to learn about the procedure beforehand, you will benefit by knowing what to expect. Knowing how to field questions from opposing counsel, as well as how to best answer questions from your own attorney at trial, allows you to exercise the self-control so critical in legal situations.

Don't wait for your attorney to call you to schedule a preparation session. Take responsibility. As soon as you find out what is going on, request a thorough preparation session, read everything you are given, and ask your attorney how you can best help with your defense. But lawsuits move slowly. It will not be necessary to call your attorney regularly to check on your case. When something develops, the attorney will contact you.

INSURERS RECOGNIZE THE NEED FOR PREPARATION

Malpractice insurers are growing increasingly aware of the importance of preparing defendant physicians, nurses, medical experts, and other health care professionals for depositions and trial. In many cases, a specially-trained consultant will be hired to work on any communication problems you may have and to increase your witness effectiveness. If your insurer recommends a special session to prepare for your deposition or for trial, take advantage of it. The few hours you spend will reap huge rewards for you, your attorney, and your insurer.

SUGGESTIONS FOR A PRE-DEPOSITION TRIAL RUN

Reading the recommendations in these chapters and practicing the exercises will help reduce your anxiety and make you feel better prepared. Another step some doctors find helpful is to conduct a question and answer simulation with the defense attorney. Responding to a range of questions you can expect to be asked in deposition stimulates recall and helps shape your thoughts into precise explanations of what you did and why. The fact that you and your attorney do not know the specific questions you'll be asked does not mean you can't prepare for many of them. It helps your attorney if you yourself prepare a list of the five or six most challenging questions you could be asked, and include these in your practice session. Remember that preparation sessions are protected by attorney-client privilege.

Video recording the session and playing back segments makes it easier to spot poor choices of words, or answers that are too expansive. Seeing yourself on video can also highlight the need for adjustments in communication style and non-verbal behavior.

Your attorney may suggest that one of his colleagues act as "opposing counsel." This increases the realism of the practice session, and eliminates any awkwardness your attorney might experience in having to conduct an adversarial cross-examination of you. Employing the services of a trial consultant for this practice session to provide feedback on listening skills and communication effectiveness is also valuable.

Practicing well-worded responses to difficult questions you can expect is a good idea, but attempting to memorize answers is not recommended. You might appear overly prepared, the question may be asked in a form different from what you expected, or you may simply forget your "canned" answer. A natural conversation flow is more convincing and more comfortable. Your goal should be to learn listening skills and question-answer techniques that are effective regardless of the specific questions asked.

While a deposition is certainly not a picnic in the park, neither is it a forced march across hot coals. Going into a deposition *prepared*—psychologically, intellectually and emotionally—reduces your anxiety, helps you feel more in control and results in a performance that will strengthen your defense.

Part of being prepared means activating your listening skills and learning how to answer questions in an adversarial context in which not only *what* you say but *how* you say it can have serious consequences. In the following chapters, you will learn the importance of a different level of listening, about questioning techniques typically used in depositions, how to recognize various types of questions, and how to give convincing, truthful answers. Remember that giving an effective deposition is one of the primary means you have of influencing the outcome of your case.

6

THE ART OF ACTIVE LISTENING

"In order to be a good witness, you must first be a good listener."

—STEVEN FITZER, ATTORNEY-AT-LAW

Most people think of themselves as good listeners. This is particularly true of physicians, trained to listen carefully to medical histories and patient symptoms. So, when an attorney advises a physician awaiting a deposition to "Listen carefully to the question before you answer it," the instruction seems straightforward. Yet active listening is difficult to carry out effectively as a witness, and it rarely occurs in depositions or in the courtroom. Most people do not listen with the focused intensity needed in a deposition. In fact, a frequent regret expressed by witnesses is their failure to listen carefully to the questions of an opposing attorney.

In everyday life, a good listener understands what the other person intends to say, not just the actual words. In a deposition, the opposite is true. All attention must be focused on the words alone, not the demeanor or the underlying emotion. This is hard to do, given years of "social" listening. Yet active listening is the best insurance you have against any attorney's attempts to manipulate or confuse you at a deposition or at trial.

WHAT IS ACTIVE LISTENING?

Active listening means hearing a question completely, from the first to the last word, understanding its meaning clearly, and remembering it long enough to respond appropriately. Over time, active listening can be tiring because of the high level of cognitive processing required. This is why counselors and speech therapists place time limits on their sessions.

Active listening is your strongest skill going into a deposition or taking the stand at trial. Without it, you will be easy prey for an aggressive attorney. Regardless of your current abilities, it is a skill that can be improved rather quickly. It begins with understanding common listening errors made by physicians during their depositions, learning ways to overcome them, and practicing.

BARRIERS TO ACTIVE LISTENING

Because we think faster than we speak, most of us engage in what communication theorists refer to as "out-listening." We listen to a speaker only long enough to determine what she is probably going to say, and then we tune out until we hear another word that recaptures our attention. In between, our minds wander. While out-listening is a time-efficient strategy in an information-overloaded world, it has a few drawbacks. Out-listening leaves you not with a memory of what the speaker actually said, but of what you *think* was said.

Another barrier is that our expectations shape what we actually hear. This is referred to as "selective" listening—hearing only what we *want* to hear and filtering out the rest. Our way of looking at a subject also shapes how much of a message we retain. It is our "mental filter" through which information is screened before it is actually comprehended. A dozen people may hear the same message—and give a dozen different versions of what was said.

Listening requires attention, and several factors can interfere with this. Time pressures, interest in the subject matter, distractions, personal styles and the sheer volume of information can affect our attention span. Our brains are efficient information processors. To avoid overload, we simply shut out extraneous data. However, what is an adaptive response in many situations will work against you in legal settings.

THE CONSEQUENCES OF POOR LISTENING

Poor listening can result in costly mistakes at a deposition or at trial. It means you may not understand a question, and thus give a false or non-responsive answer that is later used to attack your credibility. Failure to listen carefully also makes you appear uncooperative, rude, impulsive, or irresponsible. Remember, too, that in legal settings, words have great significance, and each one is recorded for later scrutiny.

Physicians who resent the time spent on non-medical business often overly anticipate questions, answer prematurely, or give information not actually requested. A question you consider harmless may contain a damaging implication overlooked in your haste. In the interest of time, you could concede a point because it is mostly true, or allow opposing counsel to put words in your mouth because you are not certain what is being asked and don't want to appear stupid. A long-winded reply to a poorly worded question could point opposing counsel down a new path and result in a longer deposition. In fact, a common defense attorney nightmare is a defendant doctor who simply can't stop talking at a deposition.

These problems are compounded by the likelihood that opposing counsel is not actively listening to your answers. Attorneys often engage in what communications expert Patrick Collins has called "challenge listening." A challenge listener is focused on formulating arguments to refute or challenge what you are expected to say. Once opposing counsel has heard the key phrases she is hoping to hear from you, there is little reason to listen further. The attorney is already preparing to challenge some portion of your response or formulate a damaging follow-up question. This is why some of opposing counsel's questions may appear repetitive. Remember that her goals for the deposition do not include listening effectively to your answers. She will later review your answers carefully when the written transcript is prepared.

RECOGNIZING PATTERNS OF POOR LISTENING

Becoming a more effective listener begins with understanding listening errors and working to avoid them. Some common patterns that work against you when being questioned by opposing counsel include:

- **Hearing only a few key words** and filling in the remainder based on what you think the attorney is asking. Some people hear only the beginning of a question because they prematurely switch from listening to thinking mode—they begin formulating an answer as soon as they get the idea of what is being asked. This can result in answering too quickly, which is difficult for the stenographer to transcribe. Worst of all, you may end up answering a question that had not been asked.

- **Jumping ahead** to the question you anticipate will be posed. Your logic is that if you answer the question you think the attorney is getting at, you can save everyone's time. Whenever you are thinking about future questions, you stop listening to the one being asked.

- **Improving bad questions** by assuming a better question and answering that one. Improving on what you actually heard is doing the attorney's job for him. Your helpful nature acts as a reflex: "That's a bad question, but I think I know what she meant, so I'll answer my improved version." Instead, you should simply ask for clarification.

- **Adding hidden meanings,** assuming malicious motives, or taking an inconsequential question too seriously. This kind of anticipation will be distracting and may arouse intrusive emotion. Avoid adding intention to a simple question.

- **Focusing on the style of delivery** rather than the actual words. If you become sensitive to the way in which a question is delivered—rude, antagonistic, sneering, overbearing—you will cease listening to the content. Questions which evoke intense emotional responses because they imply guilt or negligence can cloud your thinking. If you react to the emotion with which the question is asked, opposing counsel has achieved his objective (i.e., to throw you off balance and distract you from listening) at your expense. Unexpected friendliness, on the other hand, can be a disarming tactic to get you to lower your guard.

- **Allowing distractions** to take your focus away from listening. This is the persistent hope of opposing counsel. Thinking about an anticipated question, mentally reviewing a prior question or answer, or absentmindedly flipping through documents are common distractions to be avoided.

In reviewing these common errors, it's likely you have admitted to yourself, "Ah yes, my spouse/colleague/partner/friend tells me I do that sometimes." Simply being made aware of these listening barriers often helps to avoid them.

OVERCOMING LISTENING BARRIERS

The first step in active listening is to give full attention to the person who is talking. If your eyes are wandering, your thoughts are probably wandering. In a deposition, sit up to the table, lean toward opposing counsel, and maintain eye contact. Your posture should tell the lawyer that you are attending the deposition in a spirit of cooperation and confidence, and you will pay complete attention. This attitude automatically eases tensions.

At a deposition, be "all ears." Be a virtual *listening machine* that is actively processing every single word. Don't allow yourself to begin formulating an answer until you have heard the entire question, including the question mark at the end of the last sentence. Ask for a question to be repeated if you fear you may have missed something, such as descriptive adjectives or adverbs. Concentrate on the question being asked, not the previous one, the one you anticipate will follow, or a prior answer. Once you have given your best answer, let go of it and begin listening to the next question. Lastly, try some of the practice exercises at the end of this chapter. You may be surprised at how selective your hearing has become over time—perhaps out of necessity. Tuning up listening skills is essential when giving testimony and may benefit you in other ways, too.

TAKING TIME TO LISTEN

Your deposition is very important and nothing is gained by rushing through it. Take the time to listen carefully to each question before answering. Taking time serves several important purposes:

First, pauses give you time to put your answer in succinct form. Taking a moment to reflect on the question prevents you from blurting out an inaccurate response, cutting off the end of the question, or appearing jittery.

Secondly, if you allow a short pause between a question and answer, your attorney has time to enter an objection if it's appropriate. If a question is vague, if it has already been asked and answered, if opposing counsel failed to lay a proper foundation for the question, or if a question assumes expertise you do not have, your attorney may object. Generally these objections are for the record and you will still have to answer the question if you can. However, your attorney's objection may also contain a cue that can help in formulating a more responsive answer.

For example, an objection that a question is "vague" may be a signal for you to ask for a re-phrase, or that there may be an inaccurate assumption imbedded in the ambiguity. The point is that if you answer too quickly, objection-making by your attorney may be prevented and you may lose the opportunity for a helpful cue. This does not mean you should look to your attorney after each question in hopes of a respite from a difficult inquiry.

Lastly, pauses demonstrate your carefulness, a characteristic doctors are expected to possess. A doctor who gives a premature answer, or who only listens to part of the question, can be perceived as equally hasty in patient care.

DIAGNOSING QUESTIONS: WHAT TO LISTEN FOR

Doctors are experts at diagnosing, but they often leave these skills at the office when giving deposition or trial testimony. Just as every medical problem has a cause, a set of symptoms and a preferred treatment, each question has a purpose, a format and a preferred pattern of response. When you are actively listening, each question can be quickly "diagnosed" in order to determine the best answer. Your diagnosis should include:

1. **Is it an *open-ended* or *closed-end* question?** Open-ended questions require an explanation. An example would be: "What is your medical training?" Contrast this with closed-end questions that require only a one-word answer, usually "yes" or "no." An example would be: "You attended Harvard Medical School, didn't you?" If you tend to be talkative, open-ended questions will be your enemy. The longer your answer, the more likely you are to ramble, get confused or confuse others, utter harmful testimony, or give the wrong impression. If you tend to be talkative, practice shortening your answers using the techniques provided in the following chapter. If you are terse and agreeable, on the other hand, closed-end questions will be your enemy. Agreeing in principle in order to speed up the deposition is a common mistake. A simple "yes" or "no" is appropriate only if you agree with *every word* contained in the attorney's question.

2. **Do I clearly understand the question exactly as it is being asked?** Not every question is clear and well-phrased. However, many witnesses answer poorly worded questions or questions they do not understand because they don't want to appear foolish. Some of the most incriminating statements have been made by doctors who simply did not understand what was being asked.

3. **Is it a compound question?** Responding with a single answer to a question that contains two or more queries can be quite problematic. Imagine you were asked, "Did you know the drug you prescribed had serious side-effects, including allergic reactions, and that my client had a history of negative reactions to the drug?" What if you knew about some side-effects, but not allergic reactions? What if you knew about the possible allergic reactions but not the patient's history? A simple "yes" to the original question would be inaccurate and misleading. Whenever you face a compound question, you must break it down. A response might be, "You've asked several questions in one. Let me take them one at a time. In answer to the first part of your question, yes I knew about..."

4. **Is it a leading question?** When an attorney wants to "put words in your mouth" or "testify for you," he may make a statement and ask you to agree or disagree. Here's an example of a leading question: "So you told the nurse to call you only if the patient continued to complain of pain, isn't that correct?" He may ask the question in such a way as to suggest the answer. Another example might be this: "Would it be fair to say nurses don't call you regarding every patient complaint?" Such questions demand careful attention to ensure you are not agreeing to descriptions that are not completely accurate or too general. You will learn what to do when an attorney attempts to put words in your mouth in the next chapter on answering questions. Opposing counsel may also make a statement and stop speaking, signaling that she expects a response from you. Witnesses who are uncomfortable with silences frequently begin talking to fill the void. Expect some silences and sit through them silently.

5. **Is it a hypothetical question; that is, one that asks for opinion rather than fact?** Responding to a question that requires you to assume certain facts or conditions is much more difficult than merely stating a fact. Be very cautious. Ask whether the hypothetical applies to *all* patients, or *in this case*. Although your attorney may object to hypothetical questions, you may be forced to answer them anyway. Do not express an opinion unless it is clear that your *opinion*, not a fact, is being sought. If you cannot imagine a hypothetical scenario, or have no opinion, say so. You are never required to guess.

Some hypothetical questions can be very subtle, requiring only that you agree to assume a slightly different scene or that you add one or two additional factors in a "what if" situation. Although they appear benign, such questions can become quite menacing when later recited to jurors out of context. Consider the following example in which the defendant makes an important concession based on limited information:

Q: *Wouldn't your diagnosis have been different if you were told that Mr. Doe had abdominal pain for several weeks before his appendix ruptured?*

A: *(Not effective) Well, probably.*

Contrast this with the following response to the same question:

A: *(More effective) Not necessarily. It would depend on what kind of abdominal pain, exactly where it was located, how long it lasted, and so forth.*

In the second example, the doctor was careful not to speculate in the absence of specific information regarding the "what if" situation. This is a good rule to follow. If you are required to answer a hypothetical question, even if it appears harmless, make certain the questioner has provided enough detail for you to give a qualified answer. Otherwise, your best approach is to say you would prefer not to speculate.

6. **What type of information is being sought?** Listen carefully to the first word of each question. Questions usually begin with *who, what, when, where, why,* or *how*. Make certain you are answering only that topic. For example, don't answer a *who* question with a *why* answer, as in this exchange.

Q: *Who reviewed the chart after you left the hospital that day?*

A: *(Non-responsive) The chart wasn't available because it had been taken earlier by the attending physician.*

A: *(Responsive) No one that I am aware of.*

Tailor your answer to what is being sought—a name, a place, a time, a technique, a process, an explanation. Do not go beyond that.

7. **Is this a *provocative* question, designed to anger or intimidate?** A simple but poorly worded question asked in a sarcastic or accusatory tone can often elicit an inappropriate response. This might be valuable to opposing counsel. He may have identified one of your "hot buttons." It is important to respond neutrally to such questions. If you focus on the words, you will find it easier to disregard the tone. Keep in mind that opposing counsel is interested not only in what you say in response to a provocative question, but how you react to it emotionally. Does it "get a rise" out of you? Hot button questions can help opposing counsel identify areas in which you feel particularly vulnerable or are lacking in confidence.

8. **Am I being asked to agree with an overly-simplified statement or an inaccurate generalization?** Fearing they will appear to be argumentative, or wishing to be viewed as helpful and pleasant, some doctors will simply agree with a statement made by opposing counsel, even if it is not entirely accurate. This tendency should always be avoided. Remember that one of your goals is to be accurate, so don't hesitate to clarify a generalized statement with which you have been asked to agree. Here are two examples:

    Q: *It's important to order a hematocrit when a patient is bleeding, isn't it?*

    A: *(Not accurate) Yes, that tells you the volume of red blood cells.*

    A: *(More accurate) It depends on the how extensive the bleeding.*

    Q: *Doctors have an obligation to document important information in a patient's chart, right?*

    A: *(Not accurate) Yes, that's correct.*

    A: *(More accurate) I have a responsibility to document what is important to convey to others who are or will be providing care.*

    It would appear that diagnosing a question could take some time, resulting in long, annoying pauses. However, after a few minutes of practice with various questions, you will see how quickly you can go through the diagnostic checklist in a few seconds. Pausing for a few seconds before you answer will give you the time needed to think about your answer.

LISTENING FOR "MENTAL ALARMS"

Certain auditory signals get our immediate attention—an ambulance siren, screeching brakes, a child's scream. These signals warn us to sit up and take notice. In a medical setting, there are many such signals that demand extra attention. As a medical professional, you have learned to tune your ears for detecting such signals.

In the same way, some questions at a deposition or trial also demand extra vigilance and careful responding. When you hear certain words or phrases at your deposition, your mental alarms should go off, flashing CAUTION! CAUTION! Examples of these include:

- **Inflammatory words** and **emotion-laden** phrases, such as "negligent care," "agonizing pain," "horrific scars," "botched surgery," "prolonged suffering," "misleading information," or "inadequate attention" should raise a mental alarm. Opposing counsel may use these words or phrases to invoke an emotional response or prompt feelings of guilt and shame. They may be used in the hope that you will accept them as accurate descriptions of a situation. The use of inflammatory terms by opposing counsel must be countered by less inflammatory words in your response. Consider the following examples:

    Q: *Wouldn't you agree my client has some pretty horrific scars as a result of your surgery?*

    A: *(Less effective) Well yes, they are horrific, but not the worst I have ever seen.*

    A: *(More effective) It is rare, but not impossible for visible scars to result from surgery of the type I performed on Ms. Doe.*

    (Note the use of the term "visible" as a replacement for "horrific.")

    Q: *You provided misleading information to my client about the risks of the long term use of drug X, didn't you?*

    A: *(Less effective) I'm not sure what information she was given, but I don't think it would have been misleading. We don't give misleading information.*

A: *(More effective)* I advised her about all the material risks associated with this kind of drug therapy.

(Note that a simple "no" response might imply that you possess misleading information, but did not give it to this patient.)

Q: My client is seriously disabled as a result of your negligent care, isn't he?

A: *(Less effective)* I don't know. You'd have to ask his current physician.

A: *(More effective)* I have been told he has some mobility problems, but these have nothing to do with my care. I provided good care to Mr. Doe.

(Note that the description "seriously disabled" is not repeated in the answer.)

- **Mis-characterizations or over-simplifications** of an event or your testimony must not be allowed to stand. Such mis-characterizations, whether they are simple misstatements or errors, should be corrected with a clarifying response. If they are allowed to stand, opposing counsel will continue to use them in other questions. Following are examples of how to correct errors or distorted statements without providing more information than necessary.

    Q: For how long had my client been suffering from anemia?

    A: Ms. Doe had a hematocrit of 33.7. This does not necessarily mean she was anemic.

    (Note the defendant doctor is not accepting the characterization of the patient as "anemic" but instead supplies a concrete fact.)

    Q: What is the usual procedure for treating tendon tears like the one my client had?

    A: Mr. Doe did not have a tear in his tendon. He had a bruised tendon.

(Note the defendant doctor would have given a misleading answer had he focused only on the terms "usual procedure" and begun describing that method. His answer would have implicitly acknowledged the tendon was torn. Instead, he listened to the entire question, and corrected the mis-characterization before answering further.)

Q: *How long had you had this antagonistic relationship with Nurse Doe?*

A: *I would not characterize our relationship as antagonistic. We had disagreements and we always worked them out.*

(Had the doctor heard this as a simple "how long" question, she may have overlooked the mis-characterization of the relationship. Instead, she caught and corrected it using her own words.)

Q: *My client had a serious spinal problem when she came to see you, didn't she?*

A: *Ms. Doe was concerned about the pain in her lower back.*

(Note how the defendant took time to clarify just one word, "serious." Had he allowed this mis-characterization to pass unnoticed, opposing counsel would have used it repeatedly, and may have been successful in getting the doctor to use it also, perhaps unconsciously.)

Q: *Isn't it true you told my client the procedure was perfectly safe?*

A: *No, I did not.*

Q: *Then what did you tell her?*

A: *I told her the procedure was commonly performed and that complications were rare.*

(Here, the defendant doctor first rejected the characterization as "perfectly safe." She then resisted the temptation to give the full explanation in response to the first question. Note that the first question was technically answered with a simple yes or no. In order to learn more, opposing counsel had to ask a follow-up question.)

> Q: Didn't Ms. Doe make multiple requests for more medication to control her pain?
>
> A: As I recall, she made two requests.

(Here, the term "multiple" is ambiguous. The defendant doctor has defined "multiple" as two occasions, which is precise.)

> Q: Isn't it true, doctor, that the earlier you diagnose cancer, the more likely it is the treatment will be effective?
>
> A: The effectiveness of treatment for cancer depends on many factors; early detection is just one of them.

(Note the defendant doctor resisted the temptation to agree with the obvious. Instead, she gave a more technically correct answer without appearing argumentative.)

- **Imbedded assumptions**, if not detected and corrected, can result in a misunderstanding about your answer. The classic example is, "So, when did you stop beating your wife?" The only reply is, "I don't beat my wife." As the following examples show, it's critical to first address the imbedded assumption.

  > Q: When did you discontinue using the cannula that caused my client's infection?
  >
  > A: My use of a butterfly cannula was not the cause of the infection.
  >
  > Q: Why didn't you refer my client to a specialist sooner when you were unable to diagnose the inner ear problem she was having?
  >
  > A: I did not fail to diagnose Ms. Doe's problem. I was still gathering information and test results. I referred her as soon as the results indicated she needed a specialist.

- **Negative words** can "stick" and become the language with which an event continues to be described. The classic example is a plaintiff's attorney describing two autos colliding as a "crash," while the defense attorney refers to it as an "accident." Watch out for and replace in your answer negative words such as: *complication, severe, emergency, danger,* *traumatic, horrible, agonizing, prolonged, mistake, risky,* and *profuse*. Medical examples of negative language being replaced by more positive language might be:

> Q: *So, how long did my client suffer while waiting to be taken into surgery?*
>
> A: *We couldn't begin surgery until all the tests were completed, so he was uncomfortable for several hours.*
>
> Q: *Isn't it true my client's leg began twitching when the needle was jabbed into her hip?*
>
> A: *The insertion of the needle into the soft tissue at the hip joint was completed without incident.*

- **Absolute or indefinite words** such as *never, always,* and *constantly* can backfire if even one deviation is discovered. Replace absolute words with qualifying words such as "usually," "sometimes," "approximately," "from what I could tell," and "as best I can remember." Ambiguous words such as *frequently, slightly, generally, often, unusual,* and *numerous* are indefinite descriptions that mean different things to different people. Be certain to qualify meanings before repeating any of these words.

    Absolutes may also be buried in broad, generalized questions. Avoid accepting general statements that appear direct on the surface, but actually contain absolutes with which you should not agree. Consider this question: "Wouldn't you agree, doctor, that all patients should be completely informed of all possible risks associated with the surgery they are contemplating?" It appears obvious and straightforward. But note the use of the terms "all patients" and "all possible risks." In this case, agreement could commit you to an unrealistic norm. The response of an active listener might be: "I would disagree. Not all patients are in a condition to comprehend such a discussion, and not all risks are discussed, only the most likely ones."

- **Compound or complex queries** can include an inaccurate statement that becomes lost in excess verbiage. Long questions containing details or assumptions can distract your attention away from a key descriptive term. Look at the following examples and try to detect the hidden assumption overlooked by the defendant doctor.

Q: So, you were on call when my client came into the emergency room on the night of January 6, and you said you saw her about twenty minutes after she arrived. After you briefly looked at my client's injuries, what diagnosis did you make?

A: I concluded she had suffered a head trauma.

Q: Why was an MRI not ordered or why was she not referred to a neurologist who could have made a more thorough assessment of her severe head trauma?

A: An MRI was not warranted at that time.

Q: What are the risks, benefits and alternatives to heart valve replacement surgery?

A: Well, there are the usual risks of any surgery, the risk of infection, and the possible need for long-term anti-coagulants. The replacement valve can mis-function and need to be replaced.

The answer in the first example implies agreement that the physician's examination was brief or cursory. A more careful answer would be: "I examined Ms. Doe's injuries carefully, not briefly, and I determined she had suffered a head trauma."

In the second example, the doctor responded to only the first part of the question, and did not address why no referral was made. The physician's response also appears to concede that a less-than-thorough assessment was done and that the head injury was "severe." A more accurate response might be: "I did a careful examination of her injury and concluded it was fairly mild. An MRI was not warranted, nor was a neurological consult."

In the third example, the doctor answered only the first part of a three-part question. A more thorough answer might be: "You've asked three questions. Let me take one at a time. The major risks are…The primary benefits are…The alternatives are…"

- **Double negatives** are particularly tricky to answer. Listen carefully to double negatives to avoid being misunderstood in your response. Consider the following poorly worded questions:

Q: *Under what circumstances would you not avoid prescribing that particular medication?*

Q: *Is it within the standard of care to fail to rule out diabetes as a cause of the patient's symptoms?*

Q: *Wouldn't you say that were it not for the unnecessary surgery, my patient would not be disabled today?*

Q: *Isn't it unlikely that but for the second injury to my client's back, no treatment would have been necessary?*

Q: *So is it your testimony that you do not acknowledge that your failure to observe and record in your report the presence of a wrist fracture was not below the standard of care?*

These kinds of questions are mind boggling and it is best to ask for clarification. If you do answer a double negative question, be careful not to leave the wrong impression. A careful response to the first example above might be: "Although I typically avoid prescribing that medication, situations in which I *would* consider it include…"

- **Overly broad and ambiguous questions** may be "fishing expeditions," or they may simply be worded poorly. For example, how would you answer the following very general questions succinctly:

    Q: *Can you describe your education and training in the administration of analgesic drugs?*

    Q: *What are the hospital's policies regarding administration of morphine and other opioids?*

    Q: *What is meant by "quality patient care" in your practice?*

It's unwise to paraphrase an ambiguous question because your version may suggest ideas not considered by opposing counsel. In the following examples you can see how the defendant doctor actually helped opposing counsel formulate new areas of questioning!

Q: *Doctor, was my client better off before the surgery?*

A: *Do you mean her general condition or her ability to work?*

Q: How is acute pancreatitis treated?

A: Do you mean in general or in patients who require hospitalization?

Q: Doctor, did you conduct any research in preparation for your deposition today?

A: Do you mean literature search or some investigation of patient records?

When faced with an ambiguous question, your options are to ask for more specifics, or to give an equally broad answer. Consider these effective responses to two types of ambiguous questions:

Q: Doctor, was my client better off before the surgery?

A: What do you mean by "better off?" or

A: Can you be more specific? or

A: "Better off" in what respect?

Q: Tell me about your background.

A: I hold a medical degree from Stanford and I currently practice at West End Hospital in the OB/GYN Department. or

A: What specific aspect of my background are you referring to? or

A: It's fairly extensive. Can you be more specific about the timeframe?

Your active listening and diagnostic skills can be put to good use in a deposition or other legal settings by enabling you to quickly determine a question's purpose and format. Once that diagnosis has been made, you are in a better position to determine if clarification is needed, and to choose the best wording of your response to ensure it is accurate and specific. It is virtually impossible for any attorney to control what you say when you apply these listening methods.

TAKING LISTENING BREAKS

Active listening is tiring, and fatigue is a great enemy of active listening. Once you become tired, your attention is more easily distracted and you may short-circuit the diagnostic step. Some attorneys save the most important questions to the end, when they suspect the witness is tired and no longer listening carefully. Be aware when fatigue is coming on and get refreshed so that you are listening to the last question of the day with the same alertness you did to the first. When you feel yourself getting tired, request a break. If you are not able to take a break, don't underestimate the refreshing effect of a few slow, deep breaths.

GETTING SOME PRACTICE

Practice active listening skills with family, friends and patients. Practice diagnosing questions. Picture in your mind what a question would *look* like if it were written out. Listen to the absolutes your children often use, such as "We never go to the park!" and practice responding with more conditional terms. For just one day, try to find a word in every statement or question directed to you with which you *disagree*. Try substituting a phrase of your own. For example, if your spouse asks, "Wasn't that a good dinner we had at Doe's Restaurant last week?" you might respond, "I enjoyed the food but the lighting was too low to read the menu easily." Attempt to avoid answering any question with a simple "yes" or "no" for a few hours. It's challenging!

Another way to practice listening skills is through paraphrasing. Throughout the day, try repeating back to yourself quickly some of the questions asked of you by different people—your children, spouse, colleagues, patients. Aim for exactness. You may be surprised at how inaccurate your recall is, particularly if you are "out-listening." Paraphrase questions back to the person who asked it, as in the following example:

> *Nurse: Ms. Doe has been complaining of headaches and some nausea since her treatment this morning. What orders do you plan to leave for her?*
>
> *You: You want to know what orders I plan to leave for Ms. Doe since she is complaining of headaches and nausea following her surgery this morning, right?*
>
> *Nurse: Yes, that's what I need to know.*

Ask the person to let you know if your paraphrase was accurate. Rather than being annoyed, most people are willing to help when you explain that you are attempting to improve your listening skills. You may even enlist someone to challenge you for an entire day to be a good listener.

Another helpful practice exercise is to "read" the question being asked, rather than to hear it. Our visual comprehension is much greater than our auditory. Imagine the question being typed out in front of you on a computer screen, word by word, so you actually visualize each phrase as it is being spoken. Or imagine you are transcribing each question as it is being asked, then read the question to yourself mentally. When you are in a meeting, you may actually try writing out each word of a question or statement as it is spoken. Are there certain words, such as qualifiers, you tend to miss or leave out? Are there parts of questions you fail to hear? What do you pay closest attention to—the beginning, middle, or end of the question? Do you "out-listen" or "challenge listen?"

These exercises will promote your awareness of how much filtering and condensing you tend to apply to your communications every day. Becoming a better listener will be invaluable at your deposition, and you may find it has secondary benefits elsewhere.

7
ANSWERING QUESTIONS EFFECTIVELY

"We can judge the intent of the parties only by their words."
—SIR JOHN POWELL, ENGLISH JURIST

"A good witness is one who has the knack of answering only what was asked."
—FROM *HOW TO BE A WITNESS* BY TIERNEY

Just as there is an art to listening, there is an art to answering questions in a precise, compelling way, while avoiding many of the traps used by attorneys to cross-examine witnesses. Knowing the rules about answering questions and techniques for sidestepping "tricky" questions will help you feel more in control and less anxious.

This chapter is devoted to answering questions posed by opposing counsel, either at deposition or at trial. It is assumed that questioning by your attorney at trial should go smoothly, especially if you have prepared with your attorney in advance. However, rules for active listening apply regardless of who is asking the questions.

COMMON PITFALLS DURING CROSS-EXAMINATION

Three of the most common mistakes made by doctors in answering questions under cross-examination are:

1. Volunteering too much information or rambling
2. Poor listening, resulting in inaccurate or damaging statements
3. Loss of composure

By virtue of their training and their helpful nature, doctors want to educate others and "fix" problems. In a legal setting, this translates into being overly helpful, and giving opposing counsel more information than asked for. Add to this the desire to "tell your story" in the hope of making the lawsuit go away, and you have a formula for disaster. Many doctors talk too much, listen poorly, become angry, give imprecise replies, and answer questions they don't clearly understand. Defendants also often assume they should know everything, remember everything, and understand everything asked of them. The result is frequent guessing, assuming, and going beyond your expertise. All of these work against you.

Instead of being helpful, strive for accuracy and brevity. Instead of being overly cooperative, be cautious. Instead of being a good conversationalist, strive to be succinct and factual. Instead of guessing, strive to answer only what you personally saw, heard, or did, and what you remember clearly.

When you are not listening carefully and trying hard to be helpful, it is also easy to fall into one of the question traps opposing counsel will use to elicit answers she wants to hear. Anxious to "set the record straight," you stop listening. When you stop listening, you become easy prey for question traps. We will examine common traps in the next chapter.

Once you recognize the traps you have fallen into, you may become angry with yourself or at opposing counsel, which results in loss of composure. You may think that you are being manipulated or outsmarted. This is frustrating, and you can easily lose control of your emotions. The ability to withstand vigorous cross-examination without becoming argumentative, defensive, or angry is a hallmark of effective truth-telling. Keep your emotions in check regardless of how tiresome, trivial, abusive, or annoying you think the questions are. This can be challenging to do, but it is how the game is won.

TWO BIGGEST FEARS ABOUT CROSS-EXAMINATION

A widespread fear expressed by defendant doctors is that they will give a "bad" answer to an important question. *Bad* in this context means the answer is incriminating, misleading, incomplete, or incomprehensible. A corollary to this fear is the concern that if the question is unclear (and many physicians complain of this), the answer is also likely to be unclear. Related concerns include anxiety about appearing to be inept, fear of not knowing the answer to an important question, fear of "looking bad" to another professional, concern about memory losses, and the tension associated with being interrogated about one's care. It can also be quite frustrating to "know what you know" and not be able to communicate it. Nearly every defendant doctor is concerned at some point about how he will go about explaining the medicine involved in the case to non-medical people such as attorneys, jurors, or insurance representatives.

A second common fear among doctors preparing to give testimony is that they will be "badgered" by opposing counsel. In most cases, your attorney will object to this. But what about those situations when opposing counsel's behavior is not yet objectionable? Under cross-examination you may feel harassed or pulled into an argument you know will only reflect badly on you in front of the jurors. You may feel you are being cut off, and want to make certain you are heard. Specific statements by you, made in a respectful tone, can do much for your credibility and gain the attention of jurors. Some examples are:

> *"Counselor, you have mis-characterized the* [situation, process, testimony, event]*."*
>
> *"Counselor, you have taken that out of context."*
>
> *"You may be confused about that."*
>
> *"I believe you have misstated that."*
>
> *"Your* [question, statement, assumption] *doesn't make sense to me."*
>
> *"Counselor, I believe you have confused* [subject] *and* [subject]*."*
>
> *"That is only part of the answer, not the complete explanation."*
>
> *"I agree with you in part, but I disagree that…."*
>
> *"For good reasons, I would have to disagree with you entirely on that."*

Statements such as these, delivered with calm confidence, send a clear message to attorneys and to jurors: "I don't want to argue, but there is more to this story than meets the eye." Remember that if a lawyer is discourteous while you remain calm and collected, jurors will resent the lawyer; they will respect and sympathize with you.

CONCERNS ABOUT MEMORY

Incomplete memories can also be a source of concern to physicians, who may struggle to recall details of what occurred years earlier. Such fears are rarely justified when looked at more realistically. Unless something was significant to you at the time, it's likely you will not recall it years later. For example, some people can recall exactly where they were and what they were doing when they heard that President Kennedy had been shot, even though the assassination occurred five decades ago. Contrast this with your memory of what you had for lunch a few days ago.

The more psychologically painful an event, the more clouded the memory. Our emotional defense system tends to block out distressing events. Details surrounding the death of a patient, an extremely demanding surgery or delivery of an impaired baby are often protectively blocked from memory. Medical malpractice cases are often filed several years after the events at issue, and depositions may be taken several years after that. Even if you have a fairly reliable memory, some memory loss is expected.

Memory loss is also uneven. Your long-term memory may be better than your recall of recent events, or vice versa. It's not uncommon for similar memories to confuse your recall. Similar patients, and similar symptoms, can result in confusion about which memories are attached to which events. It's also quite possible to see a reminder and still not recall a person or event. For example, no matter how many times you are reminded about your great aunt's visit in 1984, you may still not recall much of the occasion.

There is no need to feel guilty if your recollections about a particular patient or medical situation are not perfect. Relax. When memory fails, as it inevitably will, there are several sources of information to rely on.

SOURCES OF INFORMATION FOR ANSWERING QUESTIONS

Physicians are often required to testify about their care as distant as five years after their last contact with a patient. Memories have become clouded; records appear cryptic. It is even more difficult to recall details when contact with the patient was limited to an emergency room intervention or a few office visits. It is a rare physician who can recall details of an exam or a treatment completed three years and hundreds of patients ago. How, then, can you be expected to be accurate in your recollections at a deposition or at trial?

Four Main Sources

There are at least four main sources of information you can rely on when answering questions. The first is your **unassisted memory.** You simply recall the event, the person, and the procedure as though it happened yesterday. Details make memory even more credible.

Keep in mind, however, that you may appear to have convenient "selective memory" if you can recall vividly events which support your case yet have amnesia for those that damage you. Unassisted memory was relied upon to answer these questions:

> Q: *Did you tell Mr. Doe the glaucoma could return?*
>
> A: *Yes, I did.*
>
> Q: *How do you know you told him that?*
>
> A: *I distinctly recall telling him.*
>
> Q: *How is it that you can remember Mr. Doe after five years?*
>
> A: *He is the only patient I have ever treated who lived in Bali, where my wife and I honeymooned.*

A second source of information is your **assisted or "refreshed" memory.** You did not spontaneously recall the person or event until something sparked your recall, such as reviewing the record, discussing the procedure with your attorney, or seeing a photo of the patient. For example:

> Q: *Did Mrs. Doe call you that evening to report on her husband's condition?*
>
> A: *Yes, she did.*
>
> Q: *How do you know that happened?*
>
> A: *I reviewed my patient notes yesterday and they refreshed my memory.*

The **medical record** is a third important source. Although you should be familiar with the patient's chart in preparation for your deposition, you're not expected to recall every detail of the medical records. If you do not recall the information asked about by opposing counsel, you may review the record. For example:

> Q: *At what time of the day did you perform the procedure?*
>
> A: *I don't recall the specific time, but I could tell you if I may look at the hospital record.*

The fourth source is what is referred to as your "**custom and practice.**" These are the professional routines you perform as part of your professional practice. For example, you may not recall specifically scrubbing and gloving before the surgery four years ago, but you are certain this was done because it's your custom to do so. You may not recall exactly what you told a patient before surgery three years ago, but you know you explained the procedure, reviewed the common risks, and answered her questions because you routinely do this. An answer that relies on your custom and practice is as valid as one relying on a specific memory. For example:

> Q: *Did you fully inform my client about the risks of this kind of treatment?*
>
> A: *Yes, I did.*
>
> Q: *But do you have a specific recollection of telling my client about the risks?*
>
> A: *I have no specific recall, but it is my practice to discuss the risks, benefits, and alternatives of this kind of treatment with my patients, so I am certain I did that with Ms. Doe.*

You may be challenged about whether you ever deviate from a professional practice, or how you would explain a discrepancy between what you claim to have told the patient and the patient's recollection. Be careful about alleging that you *always* give patients certain information. Remember you are testifying that your behavior was highly likely, not 100% certain. Here is a good example to how to respond effectively to a question that challenges your professional practice:

Q: *In this case, isn't it possible that you failed to do something that you contend is part of your custom and practice?*

A: *It is highly unlikely.*

Q: *But you're not 100% certain, are you?*

A: *Nothing is 100% certain but it is most likely I did it.*

THE LIMITS OF MEMORY

A cardinal rule for answering questions that rely on memory is never to allow yourself to be pushed to recall more than you actually do. Most people feel guilty about imperfect memory. The natural tendency is to "fill in" memory gaps with speculation. This can be fatal in a legal context. Focus on what you *do* remember, and don't worry about what you don't remember. If your memory is incomplete or unclear, it is perfectly acceptable to say so. There is no need to apologize. Also, while it is acceptable to refresh your memory by reviewing records, discussing events with your attorney, or mentally re-staging your procedures, it is inappropriate to *re-create* them or to allow anyone else to do that for you.

TYPICAL AREAS OF QUESTIONING AT A DEPOSITION

Every examination during a deposition is different. Attorney styles vary. Witness attributes are unique. However, some areas of questioning are common to most deposition examinations, and you should be prepared to answer. The primary questions are outlined here, but the list is not all-inclusive. Suggestions on how to answer these questions confidently are also provided, but remember they are only illustrative. Your answers must always be your own.

At trial, many of these same questions may be asked of you by your attorney, but for different reasons. Remember that depositions are taken in the *discovery phase* of a lawsuit and there is much wider latitude in what can be asked than at a trial. Even if your attorney objects to a question, you may be required at a deposition to answer anyway.

- Your medical education and training:
  Be prepared to give a brief summary such as, "I attended the University of Ohio for my degree in biology. I received my medical degree from Stanford. I completed my residency at the Mayo Clinic in Minnesota." Remember, if opposing counsel wants more detail, she will ask for it.

- Whether you are board-certified in the area involved in the case, and if not, why not:
  If you are not board-certified, say so. Do not go into an explanation of why you are not certified. Your response to a "why not" question is simply to be honest: "I am competent in my field and did not see the need for certification." or "I never had the time once I got into practice." Avoid sounding defensive—many competent physicians are not board-certified.

- Your education in the specialty area involved in the case (e.g., liposuction, laparoscopic surgery, pediatric neurology, etc.):
  Summarize this as succinctly as possible. "I was trained in liposuction in a special three-day program in 2002. I was mentored by an experienced physician who supervised six of my surgeries. I have since completed thirty-eight such surgeries on my own."

- Your relationship with hospitals, clinics, private practices, or other entities; where you have hospital privileges, your practice partners, etc.:
  Be prepared to provide a summary of this information. You may be asked about your compensation arrangement. This is done to determine if a link can be established between your compensation and the issues in the case. Be honest, but avoid unnecessarily criticizing a former colleague. Avoid lengthy explanations of why you left a practice group or why you are in a particular call group, unless asked.

- Previous lawsuits in which you were involved and the outcomes:
  Again, be as brief as possible. For example, "A patient of mine was unsatisfied with her bladder repair surgery. When it became apparent I had performed the surgery correctly, she dropped the suit." Or, "The lawsuit stemmed from the delayed identification of a small piece of material left in the wound. The case was settled for a modest amount of money." Opposing counsel will ask for more details if they are needed. The questioning attorney may be attempting to discover if there is a pattern of negligence. Usually, you are not required to report the outcome of any peer review process, as this may be confidential.

- With whom you have discussed the case:

    Opposing counsel may be searching for additional witnesses. If you discussed a procedure with a colleague, but not the case, you need not identify that person. If you have discussed the case with anyone, you may simply say, for example, "With my attorney and my spouse." Know that anyone you have discussed the case with (other than those with whom you are allowed privileged communication) is likely to be contacted by plaintiff's counsel. Ask your attorney with whom, by law, you are allowed privileged communications.

- What journals you subscribe to or what texts you consider authoritative:

    Refrain from attempts to elicit from you endorsements of any publication as an "authoritative" source. If you do, it will be difficult later to disagree with those passages from which a cross-examiner may choose to cite. Sample responses might be: "It is used often, but I don't necessarily agree with everything in it." Or, "It is one of many resources I might use." Or, "It is a good text, but in some areas, it has become outdated." Or, "I don't consider any text authoritative, as medicine is constantly evolving."

- What you have done to prepare for the deposition:

    If it is true, an answer might be, "I reviewed the patient chart (and/or hospital records) and met with my attorney." If you have conducted Internet or library searches on the medical issues, opposing counsel may ask you to provide copies of the results of your search. Your attorney may specifically request that you not conduct any literature searches. Remember that opposing counsel can ask what you have done to prepare specifically for your deposition, but not what you and your attorney have done to prepare for your overall defense.

- What you recall about the patient and the patient's history:

    Be succinct, such as, "She was a pleasant woman in her mid-thirties," or "He was a tall man who spoke with a slight accent," or "She was an elderly woman with a long and complex medical history." Be careful not to refer to the person as "the patient" or "the baby." Use his or her name, such as Mr. Doe or Ms. Doe, even if you never met the patient and only completed laboratory work or read an X-ray. If the patient is a child, use the first name or "Baby Doe." If you do not recall anything about the patient because of the time lapse, or the brevity of the contact, say so.

- Your knowledge of the medical problem presented by the patient:

    You will be asked how frequently you have previously encountered, diagnosed, and/or treated the medical issue in the case, what specific training you have had to do so, and the outcome of earlier treatments. Opposing counsel is looking for evidence that you lack competence in this area, or have had similar complications or problems in providing treatment in the past. Be honest about the extent of your experience and do not exaggerate.

- Specific case issues:

    Expect to be examined thoroughly about the specific physical or mental problem the patient presented, and your evaluation, diagnosis, treatment, and follow-up. At times, you may feel you are sitting for a medical school exam. Here is a sample exchange:

    Q: What are the signs and symptoms of encephalitis?

    A: The primary symptoms are [list].

    Q: Your note says Ms. Doe had symptoms X and Y when she saw you. Why did you fail to diagnose encephalitis?

    A: She had other, more salient symptoms. Encephalitis was on my differential diagnosis, but not at the top of the list. Her primary symptoms were more indicative of [alternative].

    Listen carefully to determine if the attorney is asking about "patients in general" or the specific patient you treated. If it is unclear, ask which. This is an important distinction when your treatment departed from usual practices. You also will be asked questions about why you did not make a different diagnosis, prescribe another treatment, or make alternative decisions about the patient's care. Remember to stay focused on what you did and why, rather than what you failed to do and "what ifs."

- What you told the patient, and when you told her:

    These questions relate to informed consent. Opposing counsel will want to know what you told the patient about the risks, benefits, and alternatives to the treatment, and when. (Remember that this is relevant only if a treatment was being considered.) You may be asked why you did not cover a specific risk or discuss a specific alternative. A typical answer is that the particular risk is not common, or that the alternative was not realistic. Remember that being asked about risks, benefits, and alternatives represents three questions, not one.

- Standard of care:
  You may be questioned about the applicable standard of care and whether you think you breached it. Remember that while you are not an expert, you are expected to know what the standard of care is for your specialty. The most truthful and succinct answer: "I used my best medical judgment in treating Mr. Doe. I did not breach the standard of care." Also, there is a difference between "standard of care" (a uniform benchmark) and professional guidelines (more advisory than compulsory). Don't be trapped into admitting a practice is a "standard" when it may be only a guideline.

- Subsequent changes in your practice:
  You may be asked what you are doing differently today as a result of the bad outcome experienced by the plaintiff. Opposing counsel is looking for alterations in procedures, policies, or treatment modalities that could reflect acknowledgement of previous error.

- Other areas unique to the situation:
  Your attorney will identify with you other areas unique to your case about which you can expect to be questioned.

CARDINAL RULES TO FOLLOW IN ANSWERING QUESTIONS

Every attorney has developed his own "do and don't" lists that guide the advice he gives defendants preparing for a deposition or testimony before a jury. If these lists were placed side-by-side, there would be a number of rules common to most, as there is considerable consensus in the legal community about what constitutes effective cross-examination testimony. Following are key principles most attorneys would agree you should follow in answering questions.

1. Always tell the truth, and stick to it.

Little white lies, exaggerations and partial truths are acceptable in social conversation, but they are completely unacceptable from a witness. You are under oath, so be as accurate as possible. The best way to cause someone to disbelieve *all* your testimony is to make an inaccurate, exaggerated, or false statement, no matter how unintended or inconsequential.

Your honesty will be challenged frequently. Opposing counsel is looking for even the smallest inconsistencies and will point them out to your discredit.

At a trial, jurors who detect inconsistencies in testimony usually disregard all testimony from that witness, and may even be instructed to do so by the judge.

One way you can be made to *appear* inconsistent is to elicit from you small concessions. If you have been questioned repeatedly on the same narrow subject, and opposing counsel does not appear to like your answer, there is a tendency to make concessions. The hope is that given a few crumbs, the attorney will move on. This would be a big mistake on your part, because a small concession will only whet opposing counsel's appetite. You will be pressed again to make further concessions. No matter how many times a question is asked, your answer must always be the same—the exact truth.

Complete honesty means you may have to concede the obvious and to occasionally admit weaknesses. Most doctors believe they must be perfect, and it is difficult to admit weaknesses. As a witness, however, you are better off admitting your small flaws. Such candor usually enhances your credibility.

2. Listen carefully and take your time.

Use the techniques covered in the chapter on active listening. Remember that to be a good witness you must first be a good listener. "Diagnose" the question being asked. Pay attention to "mental alarms" such as inflammatory and negative words, compound questions, absolutes, and attempts by opposing counsel to structure your answer in her words. Take your time. Pause briefly before answering to organize your thoughts and allow time for an objection if your attorney wishes to make one. Don't worry if your pauses annoy opposing counsel. Answering questions is not a tennis match where the object is to hit the ball back as quickly as possible. It is more like golf—slow, deliberate, and precise.

3. Do not volunteer information.

A deposition is not a seminar, and it carries no responsibility to educate opposing counsel or observe rules of social etiquette. At a deposition, it's very important to keep your answers short, precise, and focused on the specific question. Your goal is to give a "responsive" answer. This means answering the question carefully, succinctly, and precisely, with appropriate demeanor. Stay within the narrow borders of the question. Limit your answers to what you personally know, saw, did, or thought.

A rambling deposition full of opinions and tangential diatribes will reflect badly on you and may open new doors for opposing counsel. Challenge yourself to answer every question on its most basic level. Aim for an answer of ten words or less. If the attorney wants more detail, she will ask for it. Here is an example of a rambling, non-responsive answer to a question:

> Q: *What did you do when my client first came to your office after her accident?*
>
> A: *Well, first of all, you should understand that I didn't see her until about two days after the accident. She had apparently gone to the emergency room at West Hospital several hours after the accident, and then gone home with some medications. By the time she came to my office, she was in a lot of pain and was taking twice the medication she had been told to take.*

In this example, the doctor was so intent on providing background, he failed entirely to answer the question. Here is an example of a convincing, succinct answer to the same question:

> Q: *What did you do when my client first came to your office after her accident?*
>
> A: *I did three things. (Put your fingers up and tick them off.) First, I obtained some relevant history. Second, I carefully examined her arm and wrist. Third, I ordered x-rays.*

Remember that at trial your attorney will take you through a series of questions that have been prepared to "tell your story" in the most compelling sequence. At deposition, however, your goal is to be brief.

EXCEPTIONS

There are several exceptions to the rule of brevity in giving a deposition. One has to do with whether your deposition is to be read by one or more medical experts. Your attorney may plan to have an expert evaluate your treatment of the patient in part by reading your deposition testimony. If this is so, you will want to answer all treatment questions with as much detail as appropriate. Be certain to ask your attorney about this.

Another scenario relates to medical records. Your care of a patient may have been so limited there is little or no record of what transpired. In the absence of written documentation, details about what you did and what occurred will be critical. Don't hold back. On the other hand, the absence of written records is not a license to exaggerate. Restrict your answers to what you actually recall.

4. Do not answer any question you do not fully understand.

You must understand exactly what is being asked before you attempt an answer. If you do not understand a question and fail to request clarification, you cannot later rescind or change your answer, claiming you misunderstood. If you are not certain about a question, you might ask:

> *"Can you please repeat the question?"*
>
> *"I'm sorry. I don't understand your question." "Could you please rephrase your question?"*
>
> *"Your question is too general. Could you be more specific?" "I don't know what you mean by ___? Can you define it, please?"*
>
> *"I can't answer that question without more information."*
>
> *"I couldn't follow your question. Could you please ask it again?"*

Counsel can then re-state the question or abandon it. The best advice is to listen to your "sixth sense." If a question doesn't sound right, it probably needs to be clarified. Asking for clarification also puts the attorney on notice that you are listening carefully.

Questions may contain confusing double negatives ("In what instances would you not avoid that medication?") or they may simply be ambiguous ("What is your approach to patient care?"). Don't attempt to improve such questions and then respond to the improved version; just ask for clarification or greater specificity. Do not attempt to improve a poor question by answering what you *think* the plaintiff's attorney intended to ask. If you are uncertain, you might say, for example:

- *In general, or in this case?*
- *When this event took place, or today?*
- *What the general practice is, or what my personal practice is?*
- *What I know for a fact, or what my opinion is?*
- *What do you mean by "reasonable certainty?"*
- *How are you defining "standard of care?"*

It is perfectly acceptable to ask for clarification, but you should not use this as a crutch or stall technique to avoid answering a question. You should not attempt to improve the question or re-state it yourself, as in "If I understand your question, what you really want to know is..." Since you are not being paid to do the attorney's job, allow her to formulate her own questions.

5. Clarify or correct inaccuracies.

At your deposition, it is acceptable to clarify a term used inaccurately by opposing counsel, to correct misleading statements or errors, and to clear up any mis-characterizations. This can be done in the context of your answer. It is not your responsibility, however, to "educate" opposing counsel. Nor will it serve any purpose to patronize opposing counsel, or make him feel stupid. Here are some examples of how questions containing an error can be best answered without educating opposing counsel:

> Q: *While my client was anesthetized, how did you position her?*
> A: *First of all, Ms. Doe was not given general anesthetic, just a local. After the local had been given, she was put in a prone position.*
>
> Q: *So you determined he was anemic?*
> A: *I found he had a hematocrit of 33.7, which does not necessarily mean anemia.*
>
> Q: *Why did you prescribe 5 milligrams of [Drug X] twice a day for anxiety?*
> A: *The record actually reads .5 milligrams, which is a common dosage.*

6. Stay within your realm of expertise.

Sometimes counsel may want you to give testimony on a topic that exceeds your expertise. Be on the lookout for this tactic. Doctors often try to answer *every* question, whether or not they have adequate knowledge. The more intelligent and talkative you are, the more accustomed you are to having all the answers. Don't assume because a question is asked that you *should* know the answer. For example, a radiologist should not offer an opinion on the probability of recovery in a cancer patient; an orthopedic surgeon should not address the issue of future earning capacity for an injured patient. Remember that you are the defendant, not the medical expert.

7. Don't speculate or guess.

Doctors in particular are accustomed to giving opinions. To be a good deposition witness, you must put these tendencies aside. Avoid giving opinions about issues that go beyond your level of expertise, and resist pressure by opposing counsel to force you to do so. Don't be afraid to say "I have no opinion."

In a legal context, you are also not required to guess, and you should refuse to. You might say, "I don't want to guess." If forced to give your best guess, preface your answer with "I can only guess it was…"

Remember, however, that guessing at even the most minor details will get you in trouble. As a witness, every statement you make is treated like a precise statement. Don't be afraid to say simply, "I don't know."

8. Maintain volume, composure, and directness on key questions.

When you answer a question, speak clearly and fairly loudly. Adequate volume conveys confidence, and makes it easier for the court stenographer to accurately record your response. Speak in complete, conversational sentences and avoid responses which cannot be recorded such as nodding, head shaking, or "uh-huh."

Some questions, particularly key ones, are designed to "knock you off course." However, you must try to maintain your composure and answer these questions with confidence. Do not use hesitant language, such as "I think…" or "I don't believe that…." or "Let me see now…" as these weaken your response. Never preface your answer with "To be completely honest…" or "To tell the truth…" or "In all candor…" as these imply you are not always completely honest. Avoid the "Yes, but…" or "No, but…" preface, as you may not be given the chance to complete your answer.

Capable attorneys are attentive readers of body language and non-verbal cues. Dropping your head into your chest and muttering, "No, um,…I don't think, um,…that I made, um,…an error in diagnosis because, um,…" will clearly indicate a lack of confidence in your answer. When faced with a critical question, it is doubly important to look directly at opposing counsel and deliver a forceful, succinct answer. In some cases, a response even stronger than "yes" or "no" may be warranted—"Absolutely not" or "Definitely."

9. Watch your language.

Physicians use medical terms that most lay people do not understand. This is appropriate in a deposition, which is likely to be read by a medical expert who will be evaluating your care. When talking to jurors, however, the use of medical terminology appears confusing and annoying. At trial, avoid professional jargon (e.g., "surgical abdomen," "posterior thoracic," "supination") as much as possible. If you must use a medical term, give its common name or explain what it means in lay terms. Also avoid stilted language, such as "That would call for speculation on my part." A simple, "I don't know" is more effective.

Use action words: "I *evaluated…*" or "I *ordered….*" or "I *tested for…*" or "I *examined…*" rather than the passive voice such as "The patient was then examined." Use of the passive voice, or the collective "we" to describe what was done to the patient implies you are attempting to distance yourself from the patient's care or to diffuse responsibility. Use adverbs people want to associate with medicine: *carefully* examined, *thoroughly* reviewed, used my *best judgment* to decide.

Never curse or use off-color language unless you are quoting someone else. Avoid colloquialisms and slang such as "That dog won't hunt" or "Right on." Don't quote from Shakespeare or otherwise attempt to intimidate intellectually.

10. Be careful answering questions about documents.

At deposition and trial, you will be asked about various documents referred to by counsel as "exhibits." Make certain you understand who prepared them, what they mean, who had possession of them, and so forth. Always ask to see any document about which you are being asked to comment. Take time to read the document, regardless of how familiar you may be with it and despite any signs of impatience by opposing counsel. Check date/time stamps, signatures, fax headings, and other details. Then, put the document aside and ask that the question be repeated. Don't talk while you flip through a long document, as most people tend to ramble.

Don't volunteer the existence of a document. Don't agree to any requests by opposing counsel to produce documents, the results of any studies or library searches you may have done, or any textbooks. Refer these to your attorney. Don't bring any documents with you to the deposition or to court except as instructed by your attorney. Documents in your possession, including any notes you may have, are discoverable by the opposing party. Showing up at your deposition with a banker's box of documents your attorney is unaware of could put her in panic mode.

A Note on Medical Records

Written documents—medical charts, hospital records, lab reports, and operative notes—play a significant role in malpractice suits. Jurors often give written records more weight than witness testimony. Before giving testimony, make certain you are familiar with the written records you prepared in the course of your care. Make certain your testimony is consistent with those records. If your memory fails, ask to look at the documents to refresh it. Few situations are more embarrassing than to be confronted with an inconsistency between your testimony and the written record. It would be distressing to see that opposing counsel knows your records better than you do. Do not speak while examining records or documents, as you are likely to ramble.

11. Don't get angry or argumentative.

At all times, be professional and respectful. Regardless of how opposing counsel may act (and this can run the gamut from polite to flesh-eating), your demeanor should be consistently unflappable and attentive. Leave your temper and resentment at home. Getting angry with the plaintiff's attorney serves no purpose. In fact, anger is viewed as a sign of a weak case and a reaction to feelings of guilt. Negative emotion interferes with listening, thinking, and giving careful answers—your three main jobs as a witness. If things get heated, let your attorney handle it.

Remain confident but not arrogant throughout your examination. Nothing is more painful to a defense attorney than to watch helplessly as an arrogant physician self-destructs under the weight of his ego while being skillfully cross-examined by opposing counsel. Your record of past performance unfortunately carries no weight in a malpractice suit, and neither does your reputation nor the value of your real estate. On the other hand, acting meek and timid wouldn't jibe with common perceptions of doctors as self-assured and in control.

Some anger from opposing counsel should be expected, but don't respond in kind. His angry or indignant demeanor may simply be "show" for his client's benefit. It may reflect his frustration at the outcome of your being a good listener and a good witness. Don't allow the frustration of opposing counsel to throw you off course or prompt you to become defensive. Some attorneys intentionally incite witnesses because they know an upset witness is easy prey. Don't fall for it. The greatest control you exert is self-control.

12. Reflect the Four Cs: Competence, Compassion, Confidence, and Conscientiousness.

Whether at deposition or in court, you are being assessed. Sit up straight and look directly at the questioning attorney or the jury. Many people judge truthfulness by a person's ability to look them in the eye. Don't slouch in the chair, rock, or put your hands in front of your face. Organize your thoughts before answering and if it helps, use your fingers to tick off lists of things you want to say. This demonstrates that you're organized and competent. Know the chart and review the key events about which you expect to be questioned. This indicates you are prepared and cooperative.

Don't act flip or try to be humorous. Keep the volume of your speech fairly high; a low volume can be interpreted as lack of confidence. Be conversational and upbeat. Don't confuse being conversational with being chatty. Economy of words is always appropriate. However, you need not act like a prisoner of war under interrogation.

Answer all questions in full sentences. For example, when asked your name it is better to say, "My name is John Doe" than to give a curt "John Doe." Watch out for fatigue and ask for a break when you need one. Don't look at your attorney after a question is asked. This gives the impression of being "coached," and weakens your credibility. Limit the intake of caffeine and any medications that may affect your memory or speech. Never "trash" the plaintiff or the plaintiff's experts. Venting animosity only detracts from your image as a compassionate professional. Reserve anger, resentment, frustration and annoyance for private moments.

13. Listen to your attorney.

Insist on a preparation session with your attorney, and take his advice seriously. During the deposition or at trial, pay attention to your attorney's objections, as they may contain clues about the reasons he is objecting. If your attorney suggests a break during a deposition, take one. He may have picked up on something or is observing a tendency of yours that is not helpful. However, don't call "time out" too often. It could be viewed as a stall tactic, or an attempt to get coaching from your attorney.

At deposition, do as you are instructed by your attorney. At trial, do the same unless he is over-ruled by the judge. If your attorney tells you not to answer a question, stop talking. If told you may answer or that you must answer, do so, but only if the green light comes from your attorney. Never argue with your attorney at a deposition or in front of jurors. Remember that in the hospital you are the expert, but in the legal arena, he is.

IF YOU SPEAK WITH AN ACCENT

People for whom English is a second language often speak with an accent that can make communication more difficult. Accents can become even more exaggerated under stress, such as when being cross-examined. When this is coupled with low volume, rapid speech patterns, or the tendency to let sentences trail off, the result is an incomprehensible word salad. The problem can become even more serious in a courtroom, where acoustics are often poor. Jurors who cannot understand you will become impatient, and may decide to tune you out altogether. Even worse, they may conclude the patient could not understand you either.

If you speak with an accent, try the following techniques:

1. Slow down! Speak as slowly as you can.

2. Enunciate your words carefully. Practice by enunciating each syllable slowly.

3. Keep your head up and keep your hands away from your mouth.

4. Move your lips as you enunciate each word. Lip reading is a common aid. Mumbled words from frozen lips cannot be understood in even the best of circumstances.

5. Practice speaking in front of a mirror, exaggerating each of the four tips above. Speak v-e-r-y slowly, enunciating each syllable, moving your lips and talking loudly.

6. Practice saying the words "period" or "question mark" at the end of each sentence, as if you were dictating a letter. This helps to get in the habit of maintaining adequate volume all the way to the end of your sentences.

8

AVOIDING QUESTION TRAPS

"Man is the only kind of varmint who sets his own trap, baits it, and then steps in it."

—JOHN STEINBECK

A prevalent fear among most witnesses is that opposing counsel will maneuver them into agreeing with something that is not accurate or is untrue. This fear is not unfounded. Questioning witnesses effectively is a major part of a trial attorney's job, and they are well-trained to do so. While most attorneys will be pleasant and direct, some may try to intimidate you during the examination, or to limit and control your response options. If you are not aware of these questioning techniques, you could inadvertently give an incorrect answer.

Referring to the questioning strategies of attorneys as "traps" does not imply that counsel is acting illegally, or that the motives of opposing counsel are necessarily devious. "Traps" are simply one way to characterize the questioning methods used by all good attorneys (including your own) to elicit answers that best support their trial themes. Detecting a trap and avoiding it is one of your best strategies when being questioned.

Although attorney styles vary greatly, there are some basic question formats that you should be aware of, listen for carefully, and respond to effectively. The most common traps are discussed below, along with examples of how to respond. The examples are not the only answer or the "right" answer; they are examples. You must always answer questions in your own words.

COMMON ATTORNEY TRAPS AND HOW TO HANDLE THEM

The Trap: "Tricky" Questions

A question can be considered tricky if it contains one or more of the "silent alarms" discussed in the chapter on active listening. To review, questions containing any of the following could trap you into an inaccurate or misleading answer:

- Inflammatory words or phrases
- Mis-characterizations
- Imbedded assumptions
- Negative or guilt-inducing words
- Absolutes
- Complex questions
- Double negatives
- Ambiguous words or unclear questions
- Leading questions
- Hypothetical scenarios

Watch out for these traps and use the tactics discussed earlier to make certain that you clear up any errors, ambiguities, or mis-characterizations. Here are some examples of how to effectively counter tricky questions:

Q: *Weren't you very upset when you learned Ms. Doe was not improving by the next day?*

A: *I don't know what you mean by "upset." I was concerned.*

Q: *Wouldn't you agree after seeing the pictures that my client had horrific scars after your surgery?*

A: *She had developed scars that are uncommon after this type of surgery, yes.*

Q: *Can you describe the dangerous side-effects of drug X, which you prescribed for my client?*

A: *I don't know what side-effects you consider dangerous. There are side-effects to drug X, and I explained these to Mr. Doe.*

Q: *Didn't you tell the court earlier today that you never prescribe antibiotics before surgery?*

A: *That mis-characterizes my earlier testimony. I said that in cases such as Ms. Doe's, we rarely prescribe prophylactic antibiotics.*

Q: *Wouldn't you agree my client had an unacceptably poor outcome?*

A: *She had a rare, unfortunate outcome.*

Q: *What was the first action you took when you realized you had cut into the aortic valve?*

A: *First of all, I did not cut into the valve. I made a nick during surgery, which happens occasionally. I took corrective steps immediately.*

Q: *You don't remember anything about my client, Mr. Doe, do you?*

A: *I recall little about his appearance; I have a good recall of his treatment.*

The Trap: Putting Words in Your Mouth

In the previous chapter you were cautioned to listen for questions that attempt to put words in your mouth, since this is a common tactic. In this trap, the attorney may either: 1) ask the question as a statement with which you are expected to merely agree or disagree, or 2) summarize your previous testimony with her own "slant" on it. Thus, the attorney's words and characterizations, not yours, are what go into the deposition transcript.

Questions prefaced with "Wouldn't you agree that…" or "Would it be fair to say…" or "Isn't it true that…" are intended to prevent you from using your own words. At trial, such questions also restrict the communication you may have with jurors and impede your ability to develop rapport with them. Questions asking you to agree with the attorney's summary, often prefaced with "Let me make sure I understand. Are you saying [summary]?" can be inaccurate reflections of what you would say in your own words.

A simple yes or no to a question prefaced in this way might constitute a misleading answer—a half-truth or a wrong impression. You may be agreeing with a statement containing inaccuracies or words that misrepresent a situation. If you say "yes" or "no" because you agree or disagree with the attorney's statement *in principle*, you are affirming every word used by the attorney in the question.

To avoid this trap, listen to *every single word* in the attorney's statement. Only if you agree with every word should you agree. Even if you agree completely, you should avoid a simple "yes" response. To get in the habit of "speaking for yourself," answer in a complete sentence even if it means repeating the question. An example is:

> Q: *You prescribed Drug X for Mr. Doe when he was discharged from the hospital, didn't you?*
>
> A: *Yes, I prescribed Drug X at that time.*

Note that even though you have said more than "yes," you have not volunteered anything additional. What you *have* done is signal opposing counsel that you are listening carefully and will be answering in your own words.

The same is true when answering "no." If you disagree, qualify the premise using your own words. For example:

> Q: *You did not detect the mass in my client's breast when you read the mammogram taken on December 4th, did you?*
>
> A: *As I read the mammogram on that date, there was no detectable mass.*

Be careful of beginning your response with "Yes, *but…*" or "No, *except….*" You may be cut off and never allowed to provide your explanation. It is best not to say "Yes" or "No" as the first word of your answer, but rather to end with it. If you are interrupted by opposing counsel and told "Just answer yes or no," you should explain that you cannot answer the question with a simple yes or no, or that a simple yes or no would be misleading. Here are some examples of this trap and suggestions for sidestepping it:

> Q: *Isn't it true that [statement]?*
>
> A: *That is true in some cases, but not all.*

Q: *Isn't it common practice to prescribe Drug X for patients like my client who are experiencing neuropathic pain?*

A: *First, Mr. Doe did not have neuropathic pain. Secondly, Drug X is one of several commonly prescribed for the condition he did have.*

Q: *Wouldn't you agree with me that [procedure] is the preferred treatment for [medical problem]?*

A: *It depends on the particular pattern of symptoms the patient has.*

Q: *In your diagnosis, you relied on an exam and some lab reports, right?*

A: *I reviewed the results of my physical exam and the results from two blood studies, yes.*

(Note that in this example, the affirmative "yes" is reserved for the end.)

Q: *So, you're saying that after Mrs. Doe had been in labor for eight hours without significant progress, you decided to administer Drug X, because in your judgment the drug would accelerate the process?*

A: *No, that's not exactly what I'm saying. What I am saying is [response].*

(In this example, the doctor had not used the words "significant progress" or "accelerate" in previous statements and therefore would not allow the attorney's summary to stand as accurate.)

There are occasions when a simple "yes" or "no" would hasten the questioning process along, but such a one-word answer would be misleading and incomplete, such as when it is important to convey relevant context. Consider these examples:

Q: *Doctor, you never ordered an MRI, did you?*

A: *An MRI was never warranted.*

Q: *You only saw my client twice before rushing him into the surgery, isn't that correct?*

A: *I saw Mr. Doe on two occasions before we decided that surgery was the best option.*

The Trap: Inducing Agreement with General Statements

A common ploy for plaintiff attorneys is to begin a question with the implicit preface, "You would agree with me that…." Or "Isn't it true that the patient's best interests are served when a doctor…?" Such questions typically contain a generality with which it seems irrational to disagree. However, the generality itself may not be completely true. To agree is to overlook the nuances of a particular patient's care. Often a more appropriate response, for example, is, "It depends on the patient and would not apply in Mr. Doe's case." In fact, "It depends on the patient" is often the most accurate and succinct response to many general questions.

The Trap: Asking About the Standard of Care

The core of any malpractice claim is a violation of the standard of care. Getting you to admit your care did not meet the standard is as good as a confession in a criminal case. Getting you to show your lack of understanding about the standard of care is nearly as good. It is not unusual for a doctor to be hesitant to respond to questions regarding familiarity with the standard of care, as the motive of plaintiff's counsel may be suspicious. Here are several actual questions that have been posed to doctors about the standard of care, and the excellent answers given:

> Q: *Are you familiar with the standard of care for spine surgeons in the state of [somewhere]?*
>
> A: *Yes, I'm familiar.*
>
> Q: *How did you become familiar with the standard of care?*
>
> A: *It starts as a medical student and progresses through work with patients, diagnosing, learning about disease processes, employing various treatments. It's through training and experience. It is through continual learning—keeping current in your field, asking questions, talking with other doctors, reading journal articles, attending continuing education classes.*
>
> Q: *Wouldn't you agree that the standard of care requires a physician to do what is safest for the patient?*

A: *The standard of care requires a physician to exercise reasonable and prudent judgment in treating a patient. Sometimes the best treatment can involve some risk.*

Opposing counsel will know the legal definition of the standard of care, but as a physician you must have a working definition that describes what is considered reasonable under the circumstances. Don't get drawn into a legal argument about the standard; rely instead on the working definition you apply every day in your practice.

The Trap: Inviting You to Volunteer

This is often a good "fishing expedition" technique to get you to talk more and perhaps reveal something unknown to the plaintiff's attorney. An attorney delights in a witness who offers new information and/or suggests other sources of evidence.

The two methods for encouraging witnesses to volunteer information are: 1) the use of open-ended questions and 2) periods of silence from the attorney. For many people, both are invitations to talk. The use of open-ended questions, such as "Tell me what you knew about my client when she came to see you?" or "How is this type of procedure performed?" can be the open door plaintiff's counsel is seeking to uncover new areas for discovery.

Recognize this trap, and don't accept the invitation to volunteer information. If you are asked a broad question, give a short answer, or ask the attorney to be more specific. For example:

Q: *So, tell us what happened on Ms. Doe's first visit to your office.*

A: *She told me her symptoms, I took a medical history, and I examined her.*

Q: *Can you tell me about your experience in conducting an amniocentesis?*

A: *Do you mean in general, or on patients with Ms. Doe's condition?*

Q: *Tell me about your current medical practice.*

A: *I specialize in ear, nose and throat problems.* or

A: *What aspect of my practice are you asking about?*

Q: *What is your experience in treating patients with polyposis?*

A: *Your question is very general. Can you be more specific?*

Q: *How would you characterize your employment at West Health Center?*

A: *I enjoy the work and it has a good staff.*

Q: *Have you ever had problems regarding the competence of any staff at the Wellness Hospital?*

A: *Rarely.*

Q: *When you did have problems, what were they about?*

A: *They were isolated instances and I don't remember the details.*

Open-ended questions that ask you to "tell all" can also be used to freeze your testimony. In the next example, note how the attorney prevented the witness from adding anything later.

Q: *What were the symptoms my client had when she came to see you, doctor?*

A: *I remember she reported pain in her abdomen.*

Q: *Anything else?*

A: *Yes, I believe she also had a low grade fever.*

Q: *Anything else?*

A: *Um, I seem to recall she had vomited earlier in the day.*

Q: *Anything else?*

A: *No, that's all.*

Q: *Are those the only problems Ms. Doe had?*

A: *Yes. That's it.*

Q: *Are you certain?*

A: *Yes. That covers it.*

Q: *Did you consider any other possible diagnoses?*

A: *No. That was all I considered.*

In this example, should the defendant recall anything additional at trial, she could be confronted with an inconsistency. Opposing counsel might wonder aloud how it is the doctor conveniently recalled other information not recalled at the deposition. Always leave a door open on questions like these by ending with a statement such as, "That is all I can recall at this time."

The Trap: Cutting Off Your Answer

One of opposing counsel's goals is to prevent you from explaining your answers. This occurs less frequently at deposition than at trial, where every word you utter is heard by jurors and could be influential. One way in which the attorney can control what jurors hear is to "testify for you" by wording a question in a way that simply requires agreement. Another is to cut off your answer before you can elaborate. By doing so, your answer may become misleading. Consider the effectiveness, and the impact on the jury, of the following questions:

> Q: Ms. Doe's lab results were never put into her chart, were they?
>
> A: (Not effective) No, but—.
>
> Q: Just a yes or no, doctor.
>
> A: No.
>
> A: (More effective) I called the lab that day and was told her lab results, but for some reason, the written report was not put into her chart. or
>
> A: (More effective) The important thing is that I knew her lab results, even though they were not filed in her chart.

Even though the defense attorney could have come back later and clarified the doctor's blocked response in the first example, the damage would have been done. The "yes, but" or "no, but" answer is weak because it suggests you agree basically with the attorney and everything that follows sounds like quibbling. Some jurors may not hear anything that is said following the yes or no. Giving the explanation, and then ending with a conclusion of yes or no is the best tactic to avoid this trap. Note how this is done effectively in these examples:

> Q: You never followed up with my client, Mr. Doe, to determine if he was keeping his appointments with the physical therapist, did you?
>
> A: I trust my patients to follow their treatment plan regarding post-surgical appointments, so the answer is no, I did not make sure he was keeping his appointments.
>
> Q: You didn't request Ms. Doe's medical records from the physician she had been seeing in Kansas City in 2009, did you?
>
> A: I had more current information, so I did not.

The Trap: Throwing Off Your Focus

Opposing counsel may use tactics designed to disrupt your rhythm, interfere with your focus, and confuse you. Some of the more common strategies, and ways you can elude them, are described below.

The attorney speaks rapidly and keeps the pace very fast. Under these conditions, most people feel pressured to answer just as quickly. The result can be a disaster—poor listening, inarticulate answers, nervousness. Encouraged by the negative affect her pace is having on you, opposing counsel may continue to speed up. The only way to stop this vicious spin is to slow down. *You*, not the attorney, control the speed of the questioning. Set a slow and thoughtful pace for answering, and stick to it. An effective way to slow the pace is to repeat the question as part of your answer. For example:

> Q: What steps did you take to ensure adequate blood flow to Mr. Doe's foot?
>
> A: The steps I took to ensure adequate blood flow to Mr. Doe's foot were...

Opposing counsel drowns you with paper and makes frequent references to documents she has brought with her to the deposition. This tactic may be a smoke screen designed to induce you to educate her about the written record (i.e., where information can be found), or a strategy of distraction and confusion to prevent you from concentrating on questions. Don't get caught up in this tactic. Your best strategy is to: 1) wait patiently until opposing counsel has found the correct reference, 2) listen to the question involving the reference,

3) verify the information, 4) put the document down, 5) ask for a repeat of the question (if there was a long delay), and 6) answer the question. You have a right to take all the time necessary to review the document, so don't allow opposing counsel to rush you through it.

The attorney jumps from topic to topic to break your concentration, confuse you about time frames, or catch you off guard. Skipping around between subjects is frustrating because it will prevent you from completing an entire thought. Unfortunately, your insistence on being allowed to complete a "train of thought" is inappropriate and may give opposing counsel more ammunition.

While some attorneys may simply be disorganized, others use this tactic of apparent disorganization to elicit helpful behaviors from you or "wear down" your listening energy. Opposing counsel may take advantage of your disorientation by asking a provocative question when you least expect it and are not listening carefully. Take each question as it comes, even if it comes from left field.

The Trap: Asking Bombshell Questions

Some questions asked in cross-examination may hit like a ton of bricks and leave you stuttering for words. These dreaded questions can come at any time, often when you least expect them. Questions such as "What did you think when you heard Ms. Doe was permanently disabled following your surgery?" or "How do you cope with the knowledge that your failure to diagnose my client's cancer sooner has cut her life so short?" or "What did you learn from this terrible tragedy?" are designed to throw you off balance, or induce guilt. Falling into this trap means you could lose your composure, or much worse, blurt out an admission you would later regret. The only defense is to be prepared for them.

To avoid being caught off guard, practice worse-case scenarios. Before your deposition, write out the three or four questions you most dread being asked: the questions you fear you will not be able to answer adequately. Discuss these with your attorney. Here are some examples of bombshell questions and commendable attempts to respond:

> Q: *What are your feelings today knowing you played a role in my client's untimely death?*
>
> A: *I feel sorry for her family's loss, but I did not cause her death.*

Q: What have you learned from this terrible and senseless tragedy?

A: That you can give good care and the patient can still have a bad outcome.

Q: What would you say to the parents of brain injured Baby Doe today?

A: That sometimes even the best efforts aren't enough.

Q: Doctor, how do you explain how this surgery went so wrong?

A: You can do everything right and sometimes the outcome is unexpected.

Q: Wouldn't you agree Mr. Doe is justified in bringing this lawsuit, given he has lost his wife after a so-called routine hysterectomy?

A: I'm sorry he feels his loss is due to negligence, as I disagree with those claims.

Q: Wouldn't a timely diagnosis have been the best thing for this patient?

A: A timely diagnosis is important for all patients.

Q: But wouldn't you agree my client did not get a timely diagnosis?

A: The diagnosis was made as soon as we had all the necessary information.

Q: My client, Ms. Doe, is significantly impaired, isn't she?

A: I don't know what you mean by "significantly impaired" and I do not know the extent of her medical problem because I have not evaluated her current condition.

Q: If you had diagnosed Mr. Doe's cancer earlier, he would be with us today, wouldn't he?

A: In hindsight, we now know he had cancer at an earlier date. Had it been possible to detect earlier, I don't know if he would have survived it or not.

Q: What are you doing differently today to avoid this kind of negligence in the future?

A: First of all, I was not negligent. Secondly, the procedure was improved about a year ago, and I am now using the new technique because it requires less recovery time.

Q: When did you first realize your negligent care caused harm to Mr. Doe?

A: My care was not negligent, nor was it a cause of harm to Mr. Doe.

Q: You were obviously confident in your diagnosis of pelvic disease, but now Mrs. Doe is dying of cancer. Your diagnosis was totally wrong, wasn't it?

A: Given what was known at the time, my diagnosis was clinically sound.

Q: Wouldn't you agree my client had an unacceptably poor outcome from your surgery?

A: She had a rare, unfortunate outcome.

Q: This kind of bad outcome does not occur if a doctor uses reasonable care, right?

A: Although this outcome is rare, when it does occur, it is often due to the inherent risks of the procedure.

Q: How do you feel knowing my client is now confined to a wheelchair?

A: It is sad whenever anyone has a bad outcome, but his condition is not the result of the care he received from me.

Q: Didn't you tell my client you were sorry for what you had done when you visited her prior to her discharge?

A: I don't recall saying that. I most likely said I was sorry that she had an unfortunate outcome.

Note in these examples that the goal is to reflect your compassion without admitting guilt or personal culpability. It is that balance that leaves a positive impression on jurors, too.

The Trap: Pointing Out Inconsistencies

By pointing out that your testimony is at odds with the testimony given by others, the attorney hopes you will concede that you are in error, or that you will change your testimony. Plaintiff's attorney may read from someone else's deposition, quote from an "authoritative" text, cite an expert's opinion, or quote her client's allegations. If your position is true to the best of your knowledge, stick to your guns. Don't be intimidated.

Opposing counsel may also try to throw you off balance by pointing out an inconsistency between something you said earlier in the deposition and your response to a current question. If you think the attorney has mis-characterized your earlier testimony, ask that the previous question and answer be read back to you. If the attorney has in fact detected an inconsistency, now is your chance to clear it up by saying, "I'm sorry. I misspoke earlier," Or "What you have just asked me is a slightly different question."

Regardless of the importance of the inconsistency, avoid calling into question another witness's honesty. If your recollection of an event differs from someone else's, it is up to a jury to determine whose recall is more likely. Use tact and "take the high road" when confronted with inconsistencies, as shown in these answers:

> Q: *Dr. Smith, who assisted you in surgery, said he could not see the tendon at one point in the operating procedure. You have testified you had it under constant visualization. Are you saying he isn't telling the truth?*
>
> A: *Actually we are both correct. He could not visualize the tendon from his position at the operating table, but I could from my position.* or
>
> A: *I'm assuming everyone is telling the truth. Our recollections of the events are different.*

Q: *How can you be so certain Mr. Doe didn't say anything about the increasing weakness on his left side?*

A: *If he had reported that kind of symptom, I would have noted it in his chart.*

Q: *Didn't you tell us earlier that you do not note everything in the patient's chart?*

A: *I would have noted something like that.*

The Trap: Repeating the Same Question in Different Forms

When an attorney is unsatisfied with an answer, he may pose the question in a different way, hoping to elicit a "better" answer, or one more supportive of his case. He may ask the same question several times, with slight variations, in the hope you will create an inconsistency. He may do this to the point of becoming annoying. He may re-phrase the question slightly or appear to be "splitting hairs" in the wording of the question. He may preface the re-worded question with an intimidating or condescending remark, in the hope of angering you into a different answer. This tactic will try your patience, but stick to your strategy of consistency. Treat every re-phrase of a question as a new question.

It is best to give the same answer, no matter how many times the same question is asked. You might reply, "I think I have already answered that question" in a pleasant but firm tone. Here is an example of a series of questions designed to elicit some concession on the part of the doctor. Note how the witness's perseverance foiled the attorney's tactic.

Q: *What time did you arrive at the hospital that evening?*

A: *Between 8:00 and 8:15 PM.*

Q: *Could it have been as late as 8:45?*

A: *My recollection is between 8:00 and 8:15.*

Q: *But it could have been 8:45, couldn't it?*

A: *My recollection is between 8:00 and 8:15.*

Q: *Perhaps you're not listening to my question. I asked if it was possible the time could have been 8:45.*

A: *My recollection of the time was between 8:00 and 8:15.*

The Trap: Embedding Dangerous Assumptions

Embedded assumptions are "blind spots," and they are dangerous because we are usually unaware of them. They can be overlooked when you are not listening carefully or when you are listening only selectively. Like a high-speed baseball pitch, an embedded assumption can fly right past you.

Here are some examples of thorny questions with embedded assumptions, and sample answers that tell opposing counsel, "I'm listening!"

> Q: *In what ways were hospital policies violated when you administered morphine after giving Percocet to Mr. Doe?*
>
> A: *There are no hospital policies with regard to this. There are guidelines and clinical judgment.*
>
> Q: *How many times did you see Mr. Doe regarding his foot wound infection before rushing him to surgery?*
>
> A: *I didn't rush him to surgery. We met and I examined him several times before deciding surgery was the best option.*
>
> Q: *How many other times in the past have you had a complication when injecting steroids such as Mr. Doe received?*
>
> A: *I didn't have a complication with Mr. Doe's injection, so the answer would be none.*

The Trap: Focusing on Your Failures and Omissions

Getting you to admit you failed to perform some test or treatment, or that you engaged in some substandard practice, can be devastating. Questioning techniques that induce self-doubt and undermine confidence can result in an inadvertent admission on your part. Such tactics are used frequently by questioning attorneys. Don't be thrown off guard by this approach designed to make you feel guilty, inadequate, or incompetent.

Asking why you did not chart something, why you did not order a certain test, why you did not start a treatment sooner, why you did not choose another surgical technique, or why you did not consider other diagnoses, puts you on the defensive. Once on the defensive, it's difficult to avoid sounding argumentative and self-protective. When that happens, you may stop listening and begin formulating defensive strategies to convince opposing counsel of your innocence. The end result is that you lose, and opposing counsel wins.

The most effective strategy for avoiding this trap is to follow grandmother's advice: "When all you have are lemons, make lemonade." When confronted with statements about what you failed to do, use the opportunity to talk about what you *did* do. Look at these examples of turning lemons into lemonade:

> Q: You didn't administer prophylactic antibiotics to Mrs. Doe prior to her delivery did you?
>
> A: Prophylactic antibiotics are rarely administered under Mrs. Doe's circumstances. I did check to make sure her blood cell count was not abnormally high.
>
> Q: You didn't ask Mr. Doe about his prior experience with this drug, did you?
>
> A: I took a fairly thorough medical history and he did not mention any negative experience with it.
>
> Q: You've heard the adage that if it isn't in the chart, it didn't happen, haven't you?
>
> A: I heard that in medical school, but it is not necessarily true.
>
> Q: Well, there is no chart note about the conversation you claim to have had with Ms. Doe. How do we know it ever happened?
>
> A: Not everything I do with a patient or every conversation we have is documented in the medical chart, but it is my routine to hold this kind of conversation with my patients prior to vascular surgery. or
>
> A: I have many conversations with my patients. It would be impractical to chart all of them.
>
> Q: You didn't administer Drug X to Ms. Doe, did you?
>
> A: It was not indicated. I did have the nurses elevate her feet and apply moist compresses every hour.

Q: You didn't order an MRI for Mr. Doe, did you?

A: No, I did not.

Q: Even though you knew he had a serious back injury, you still refused to order an MRI?

A: After careful examination, I determined an MRI was not necessary.

Q: You didn't note her temperature in the chart when you saw her that day, did you?

A: We don't chart the absence of symptoms. I remember checking to see if she was flushed or felt hot to the touch and I asked her if she had experienced any fever. Both were negative.

Q: You never told my client he could suffer from aphasia as a result of the surgery, did you?

A: I did not discuss that symptom, as it is rare. I did discuss the common risks and asked if he had any questions.

Q: Why didn't you tell my client she would have vision loss after her surgery?

A: I did explain to her the drawbacks of this surgery, including the possibility of vision problems. No one can predict the type or degree of vision loss, if any.

Q: Couldn't you have called in a specialist while the patient was still in the hospital?

A: If the services of a specialist were required, yes. There was no apparent need for one in Ms. Doe's case.

The Trap: Probable versus Possible

There is an important difference between the legal implication of "probable" and medically "possible." If a situation or event is *probable*, it is likely to happen, exist, or be true; there is a very high chance of occurrence. An event or situation that is *possible* may happen, exist, or be true, or it may not. Once you admit that an event or outcome is probable, you will likely be asked the follow-up question: "How probable would it be that [event or situation] would occur?" In some cases, opposing counsel may be seeking a specific percentage or range of percentages. It is best to avoid the arena of probability altogether, such as in the following examples:

> Q: What is the probability that if the diagnosis had been made sooner, my client would not have suffered permanent nerve damage?
>
> A: It is possible that an earlier diagnosis would have resulted in less nerve impingement, but we can't know for certain.
>
> Q: How probable is it that my client's cancer will reoccur within the next five years?
>
> A: I don't know the statistics regarding recurrence rates. A recurrence of cancer is an unfortunate possibility.

The Trap: Making the Inconsequential Appear Monumental

This tactic of "making mountains out of molehills" may be used to sidetrack you into thinking the attorney knows something you don't. The issue will take on greater significance if your reaction dictates it. These queries are often made simply to gauge your reaction. Opposing counsel may ask a question as if he knows something that you do not, hoping to trick you into self-doubt or feeling guilty. You are left wondering if facts have been uncovered that implicate you. Your answer then sounds defensive.

Minor or insignificant events should be treated with the minor reaction they deserve. Remember that not every question may be important or relevant. This is especially true in depositions, since they take place during the discovery phase. In trial, an irrelevant question will raise an objection. Here are some examples of this trap:

> Q: So, you didn't test for diabetes when you saw Mr. Doe, did you? (Implication: You overlooked something important.)
>
> A: That is not something we would normally test for.

> Q: Are you telling me you can complete nearly two dozen of these surgeries in one day? (Implication: You do these so fast you are undoubtedly making errors.)
>
> A: It is a very routine procedure that I am very good at. Usually each surgery requires less than 20 minutes.
>
> Q: You stated earlier you had a meeting to attend immediately following my client's appointment with you. Is this correct—did you attend a meeting that afternoon? (Implication, you were in a hurry and forgot to make an important chart note.)
>
> A: When I had finished the office visit with Mr. Smith, I wrapped up some paper work and then left for a meeting about 20 minutes later.

The Trap: Enticing You to Point Fingers

It is tempting to point fingers at others in order to limit your own liability and distance yourself from claims criticizing the care provided. Plaintiff attorneys know that by blaming others for what is claimed to be substandard care, you may not only be jeopardizing a strong, cooperative defense, but also diminishing your credibility as a responsible professional. They may attempt to entice you into a blame game, or throw co-defendants under the bus, a tactic that takes advantage of our natural tendency to defend ourselves by shifting blame. If not detected and combatted, it can have the boomerang effect of reflecting poorly on you.

One of the most effective ways to deflect attempts to entice you to point fingers is to focus on *roles* rather than specific actions. Note in the following example how the doctor avoiding claiming the facility was to blame for the absence of records in his file.

> Q: The mental health center failed to send you their records of the patient's care at their facility, right?
>
> A: As the primary care provider, I expected the facility to inform me of anything relevant to my care. That does not always involve sending records.

NO ONE IS PERFECT

Recognizing and avoiding various traps used by questioning attorneys to elicit incriminating answers is a major step in taking control of your testimony. The traps discussed in this chapter can be avoided if you:

- Listen carefully to every word of a question
- Formulate each answer in your own words
- Remain calm

However, no matter how actively you listen to a question, and how accurately you diagnose it, not every answer you provide will be perfect. Don't risk the distraction of "Monday morning quarterbacking" each answer you gave; don't berate yourself the next day for answers you considered less than satisfactory. Reading this guidebook will increase your effectiveness many-fold, but you must realize that few, if any, witnesses give perfect testimony.

A LAUNDRY LIST OF THINGS TO AVOID

While it is most important to focus on positive action, there are some "do not's" when giving testimony. Here are some things to avoid:

- *Avoid* using negative words such as: risk, damage, problem, error, fault, guilt, shoddy, careless. Replace them with positive terms such as opportunity, potential, safe, thorough, careful, fair, sound.

- *Avoid* using terms-of-the-trade or acronyms without explaining them, and avoid communication patterns unique to the medical environment. For example, do not say, "The patient presented on Tuesday." Say, "She came in to the office on Tuesday."

- *Avoid* denying the obvious. Asking a simple question in a sarcastic tone can induce some witnesses to deny the obvious or even lie. This will only distract from your credibility. One popular question that tends to elicit a defensive response is, "You're not board certified, are you, doctor?" This throws many doctors into a long, defensive explanation when a simple response is more appropriate: "No, I'm licensed but not board certified."

- *Avoid* using titles such as "sir" or "ma'am" in addressing opposing counsel. These military salutations are inappropriate except where rank applies. Address counsel by his or her name (Mr. Jones or Ms. Smith) or as "counselor."

HANDLING DIFFICULT SITUATIONS

No matter how experienced you may be or how well you prepare to give testimony, difficult situations may arise that require quick thinking. Here are some responses you may find useful in certain situations.

If this happens…	Try this…
Opposing counsel won't allow you to complete your answer, or restricts your answer.	"May I please finish my answer?" "If you restrict me to a yes or no response, I can't answer your question completely."
Opposing counsel loses her composure and begins to badger you.	Remain cool and collected. It could be a trap to induce you to become emotional and stop thinking.
You begin to lose your composure and become argumentative.	Take a break. Get some air. Remind yourself that if you lose your cool, you lose overall.
Opposing counsel begins asking about what you and your attorney have discussed.	Counsel may be violating attorney-client privilege. Look to your attorney to decide if the question can be answered. Do not answer unless your attorney allows it.
Opposing counsel asks you for a document believed to be in your possession.	Look to your attorney to respond. Opposing counsel has a right to see any document, so bring only what your attorney has instructed you to bring.

If this happens…	Try this…
Opposing counsel asks you a hypothetical question, beginning with "Let's suppose…".	"I'm sorry, but I cannot imagine that scenario"
Opposing counsel misstates your prior testimony.	"You misstated what I said earlier. What I said was…". Ask the stenographer to read back your previous answer.

A Few Reminders

1. Don't hide behind "I don't know" or use it to avoid answering a challenging question.

2. Medical records will be important. Be very familiar with them, particularly those that relate directly to your care. Know where in the medical record to locate important information related to your care, but don't attempt to memorize it.

3. Avoid criticizing other doctors or hospitals. This reflects badly on you and the medical profession. If you are asked to give an opinion, offer it only if you have one. Make certain it is clear that it's a personal opinion. If asked why another doctor disagrees with your position, you might say, "Our experiences have been different" or "We simply disagree on that point."

4. Do not be coy, sarcastic, or play word games in an attempt to match wits with the attorney. Do not attempt to outsmart opposing counsel. She will always know more law than you will. In a battle of egos, no one wins.

5. Don't hesitate to discuss patient responsibility. For example, "I trusted Mr. Doe to call if there were any problems." or "I assumed Mr. Doe would give me a complete history when I asked about prior injuries to his hip."

6. Remember to watch your posture, volume, and nervous gestures. These non-verbal behaviors can speak volumes to an opposing attorney, and especially to jurors.

7. Get a good night's sleep and a good meal before your deposition. Try to avoid "On-Call" duty the night before.

A TEST OF YOUR DIAGNOSTIC SKILL

So far we have focused on how to listen to questions in order to diagnose and then avoid potential traps. Let's put your new skills to the test. Listed below are twelve questions, eleven of which contain one or more traps. See if you can detect the traps, as most of the questions contain more than one. You will have an advantage because you are reading rather than hearing the questions. Using your newly learned skills, how would you best respond? The correct "diagnoses" and some sample responses follow the list. Keep in mind these are fictitious questions. We are guilty of some over-analysis in intending to make our teaching points. The intent is to get you thinking as a careful "question diagnostician."

Questions

1. As a family practitioner, how much less skilled are you than a pediatrician in diagnosing cardiac problems in children?

2. Doctor, isn't it true that my client, Mr. Doe, was actually better off before you performed surgery than after?

3. How do you treat femoral neuropathy?

4. Of all the steroid injections you gave last year, how many resulted in complications?

5. Can you tell me about the staff problems the health center had in 2011 and why those problems caused you to leave?

6. Isn't it a radiologist's job to detect all abnormalities on X-rays?

7. What did you tell John Doe about the complications he might have after the chemotherapy and how these complications could be managed?

8. Wasn't it careless of you to undertake such a risky procedure when there were more conservative measures you could have taken first?

9. It's been a long time since you saw Mr. Doe so you're no longer certain about what your brief exam revealed, are you?

10. Who sets the policies in your clinic about which patients need to be seen immediately?

11. What is your professional address?

12. Do you have any other opinions related to this case that you have not told me about today that you wish to get on the record?

Suggested Responses

1. This question contains the imbedded assumption that you are "less skilled" and thus less able to diagnose a potential cardiac problem. There are several potential replies:

> A: *The skills of a pediatrician and a family practitioner are specialized in different areas, but one is not more or less skilled than the other.* or
>
> A: *I am less specialized than a pediatrician, but my medical training and experience enable me to diagnose cardiac problems, including those in children.*

2. This question contains several traps. First, its structure is an attempt to put words in your mouth and require only a "yes" or "no" response. Secondly, it contains a very ambiguous phrase, "better off." Potential replies include:

> A: *What do you mean by "better off?"*
>
> A: *If you mean by better off, was she in less pain, my answer is no. The surgery reduced her pain considerably.*
>
> A: *No, I would not agree that she was better off before the surgery. She was having chronic pain and could barely walk into my office.*

3. A defendant could spend a day answering this broad, open-ended "fishing expedition" question. Its intent is to get the defendant talking on record so opposing counsel can later compare the doctor's treatment approach to that of his experts, elicit qualifications that make the defendant doctor appear loose-lipped, or merely assess how talkative she is. The way to respond is with a broad, non-specific answer, such as:

> A: *It depends on the cause and other factors.*
>
> A: *There are a number of ways it can be treated.*

4. This question has several traps. It contains an embedded assumption and several ambiguities. First, it is not clear whether the attorney is referring to all injections you gave last year, or only those given at the same site (spine, knee, etc.) as the patient in this case. Second, it's not clear what she means by "complication." Lastly, it includes the assumption the defendant doctor faced *any* complications. An effective response might be:

> A: *Do you mean all steroid injections or only those of the type I administered to Ms. Doe?* or
>
> A: *What do you mean by "complication?"*
>
> A: *None of the steroid injections I administered last year resulted in any patient complaints.* (Note in this answer the defendant doctor defined "complication" as patient complaints.)

5. This clumsy but clever question lays several traps. First, it may be asking you about issues you know little about, but which opposing counsel may hope you will speculate on. Secondly, it assumes that you left the organization because of certain problems, which may or may not be true. Lastly, it is a compound question and contains more than one query. The attorney's hope is that you will launch into a dissertation about all the problems that prompted you to leave. Here are several suggested responses:

> A: *You asked two questions. Let me answer the first part. I was aware the clinic was having difficulty retaining pediatric neurologists, but I do not know the details. Secondly, my leaving the clinic in 2012 was not due to any staff problems.* or
>
> A: *You have asked several questions in one. Which one would you like me to address first?*

6. This question appears straightforward, but it has two traps: it is basically an oversimplification and it contains the absolute "all." Agreement with this question could paint a defendant doctor into a dangerous corner. Suggested answers:

> A: *The reality is that not all abnormalities are detected. It is a radiologist's job to detect with as much accuracy as humanly possible.* or

A: *It is the radiologist's job to detect as many as possible, but not all abnormalities are detectable on an X-ray.* or

A: *No, it's impossible to detect ALL abnormalities.*

7. Again, this is a two-part question. By now, you should be handling these with ease. Inadvertently, the attorney has left you an opening to say something positive about your care of Mr. Doe. Did you recognize it? Here is one example of how a defendant might respond accurately, and also score some extra points:

A: *You've asked a two-part question. Let me answer in two parts. First, I discussed the material complications of chemotherapy fairly extensively with Mr. Doe and answered his questions. Secondly, we talked about how we could best manage some of the more common complications if they came up. Mr. Doe was well informed about his treatment.*

8. This question's main purpose is to inflame you by using words like "careless" and "risky." The knee jerk response to this question could easily be some form of "How dare you insinuate!" Here, a calm and careful response is in order, such as:

A: *Your question completely mis-characterizes the situation. The procedure I recommended to Mr. Doe was not risky; it is actually relatively safe in men of his age and condition. I suggested it only after Mr. Doe told me he was not satisfied with the other treatments he had tried. I consider myself a careful physician and I typically take conservative measures first.*

9. Although appearing fairly innocent-sounding, this question is attempting to put words in your mouth. A "yes" or a "probably" answer could be very misleading. What is meant by "a long time?" What is meant by "no longer certain?" What is meant by "brief" exam? This question is less problematic than most, because a thoughtful answer can clear up the ambiguities. For example:

A: *It has been two years since I examined Mr. Doe but I have had an opportunity to review my records and refresh my memory. I conducted a thorough physical exam when I last saw him and the records indicate that other than a slight elevation in blood pressure, the results were unremarkable. He appeared to be in good shape.*

10. Hearing this question, most defendants would likely have allowed the term "policies" to slide by. Policies can be loosely or stringently applied. But remember that in giving sworn testimony, every word is important. This kind of question can also spark a rambling answer about your practices, the various exceptions that are encountered, and so on. A precise answer might be:

> *A: No one. We have no "policies" in terms of having anything in writing about how to handle potential emergencies.* or
>
> *A: No one really sets the policies because our practices are more like guidelines than strict policies.*

11. Unless you are completely obsessive at this point, the question contains no traps. Be careful not to overanalyze questions to the point of insisting the attorney define what is meant by "professional."

12. This is a great "fishing expedition" question and it is surprising how often this kind of open-ended, last-minute inquiry actually elicits a wordy response, much to the chagrin of defense attorneys. Even if you have some insightful opinion or brilliant comment to make, you do not want it on the record. Nor is this the place to launch into an extended explanation of why you believe the lawsuit is baseless. The only answer to a question like this is "No."

9
WINNING DEFENSE STRATEGIES

*"What is of supreme importance in war
is to attack the enemy's strategy."*

—SUN TSU, FROM *THE ART OF WAR*

Just as malpractice defense attorneys refine over time various strategies to strengthen their cases, counsel for plaintiffs are also continually developing strategies and innovative theories around which to build their cases. Understanding some of the more common theoretical perspectives and jury-centered themes of plaintiff attorneys can provide a foundation for effective counter-strategies for the defense. Defendant healthcare professionals who are aware of both plaintiff themes and defense counter-strategies have a better grasp of the "big picture" and will likely be more effective and persuasive in giving testimony at depositions or at trial.

In the first part of this chapter, several of the more prevalent plaintiff strategies are summarized, along with possible reasons of why they may have inherent appeal for jurors in medical negligence trials. The second half of the chapter includes common counter-arguments that have been used effectively by defense attorneys. There are also suggestions on how to respond to questions during a deposition or at trial that may arise from plaintiff's new (and not-so-new) legal themes in medical malpractice cases.

COMMON PLAINTIFF THEORIES

The following theories or trial themes are among the more common arguments made by plaintiff attorneys to shape their clients' cases. They are not all-inclusive, but are rather intended to give you an idea of the potential underlying premise of a plaintiff's case. You can expect these themes to emerge as plaintiff's counsel takes your deposition and questions you at trial.

Failure to "Rule Out" Life-Threatening Conditions

A very common plaintiff theme is to argue that in constructing a differential diagnosis, the doctor failed to consider a life-threatening condition, and/or failed to take steps necessary to rule out a dangerous potential cause.

This theory has inherent juror appeal because it relies on commonsense logic: If a symptom is connected in any way to a life-threatening condition (for example, chest pain as a symptom of a heart attack), the condition should be at the top of the differential and the doctor must do everything possible to either treat the condition immediately or take all steps necessary to rule it out. To do otherwise is to be negligent.

Appeals to the Basic Needs of Jurors: The Reptile Brain

In an interesting application of neuropsychology to the jury system, Ball and Keenan, in their book entitled *Reptile: The 2009 Manual of the Plaintiff's Revolution*, advocate trying plaintiff cases by aiming appeals at jurors' primitive drive for personal safety and security. By framing arguments in terms of one's most basic need for safety, and thus appealing to a juror's "primitive, reptilian brain," plaintiff attorneys are urged to portray a physician's negligent conduct (or lack of action) as a threat to the juror's own safety and the safety of one's community.

The notion that the greater the danger, the more the reptile cares is a simple and memorable theme. Engaging jurors in this way, plaintiff's counsel frames the case in a way that is designed to affect them personally, evoking an emotional response to the issues in the case, rather than a rational one. Reports from the plaintiff's bar suggest that used effectively, this fear-based approach has produced damage awards for plaintiffs in the millions. The theory has mobilized plaintiff attorneys, unified a strategic vision, and built their confidence in taking lawsuits to trial.

While the scientific basis for the reptilian theory has been challenged, it is quite likely that physicians and other healthcare professions being deposed may be subjected to questions based on this idea. Such questions tend to focus on the safety of medical treatment and procedures, and the provider's responsibility to ensure the safety of patients. Some queries may include generalizations which seem quite reasonable at first glance. Questions such as, "Isn't it true that a doctor's first responsibility is to ensure the safety of his or her patient?" or "Isn't patient safety the first priority when caring for a patient?" appear to warrant an implicit "yes" response. Affirmative answers are typically followed by questions which explore various aspects of your care that may have compromised patient safety. These inquiries are intended to lead you to an admission that you violated the number one rule of medical care—patient safety. Even the best-prepared physicians can be thrown off course if they are not prepared for this kind of questioning.

Violations of the Standard of Care

As discussed earlier in this guidebook, the basic claim in medical negligence lawsuits is that the physician violated the *standard of care* in treating the patient. In other words, the physician failed to exercise the degree of skill, care, and learning expected of a reasonably prudent doctor in a similar specialty, acting in the same or similar circumstances at the time of the care or treatment in question. In fact, the legal definition of negligence is the failure to follow the applicable standard of care.

Plaintiff attorneys often attempt to connect standard of care directly to the outcome of a medical procedure, and argue that because there was an undesired outcome, there must have been a violation of the standard of care. This route is referred to by defense attorneys as "hindsight bias" or using a "retrospect-o-scope," and it overlooks the fact that the standard of care relates to the treatment involved, not just the outcome. An unfortunate outcome does not mean necessarily that there was a breach of the standard of care.

One popular strategy for making the case for a breach of the standard of care is for a plaintiff's attorney to present the defendant doctor with a list of actions the standard of care required in the case at issue. The list may be constructed with a box next to each action item representing "yes" or "no" under the heading "Was This Done?" Since the concept of standard of care is often difficult for jurors to grasp, this alluring approach can render the concept more concrete and measurable for them.

A similar approach is to reduce the standard of care to a question of whether the healthcare provider violated the standard of care by failing to comply with the policies and/or procedures of the facility in which the care occurred—a hospital, clinic, laboratory, etc. A violation of these "standards" is claimed to constitute negligence in a legal sense. Plaintiff attorneys may even argue that charting errors or omissions represent violations of "charting standards of care."

Negligence as a Violation of Medical Rules

With their books, *Rules of the Road* and *Winning Medical Malpractice Cases*, attorneys Malone and Friedman have also had a significant impact on how plaintiffs present their legal cases to juries.

A basic technique in "The Rules" approach is to draw an analogy between the rules of roadway driving and the "careless or reckless" behavior the doctor engaged in when treating the patient. Suggesting there are basic rules for medical care that are as easy to understand as a speed limit sign, the approach is straightforward—doctors who violate the rules of good care should be held accountable much like a person violating traffic rules.

Appealing in this way to simple commonplace guidelines, plaintiff's counsel makes the leap to arguing the physician violated the "rules" (i.e., standards of care) to be followed by healthcare professionals. The following rules checklist is an example of the kinds of questions you may be required to answer in a deposition or at trial regarding potential rules violations. In some cases, you may be given the checklist and simply asked to complete it. The completed checklist can then be entered into evidence at trial and perhaps used to impeach your testimony if you later wish to modify a response.

THE RULE	Physician's Response
A physician must form a differential diagnosis of the potential causes of a patient's condition.	Yes ☐ No ☐
In forming a differential diagnosis, a physician must rule out the most dangerous potential causes first.	Yes ☐ No ☐
A physician will use all reasonable means to rule out a danger to a patient.	Yes ☐ No ☐
A physician will perform all reasonable tests to rule out a danger to a patient.	Yes ☐ No ☐

A physician will timely consult all reasonable specialists required to rule out a danger to a patient.	Yes ☐ No ☐
When there are several ways to treat a patient, a physician must always choose the safest way.	Yes ☐ No ☐
To not follow one of more of the above rules needlessly endangers a patient.	Yes ☐ No ☐
To needlessly endanger a patient is negligent.	Yes ☐ No ☐

Notice two aspects of this approach that can easily trap an unsuspecting defendant doctor. First, the response options are limited to "yes" or "no," thus precluding a potentially more complete answer that may provide important context. Secondly, the use of the qualifier "reasonable" implies it would be irrational to disagree.

Communication Breakdowns Between Medical Personnel

When argued effectively by a plaintiff's attorney, it is relatively straightforward for jurors to conclude that the professional whose care is at issue had the same drawback as the jailer and prisoner in the movie *Cool Hand Luke*—a failure to communicate. This can be a powerful and effective theme for plaintiffs, particularly in today's environment. Text messaging, tweeting, and social networking sites encourage and promote not only immediate information exchange, but also what might be considered excessive communication. In today's world, communication seems not only easy and prevalent, but necessary.

Using a list of what should have been communicated, plaintiff counsel argues how the outcome would have been much improved if the providers had simply made more notes in the medical chart, spoken more often to each other during the period of care, or made the effort required to be completely informed of the patient's progress. This taps into common expectations that information exchange is a critical component of good patient care. The inherent appeal in this strategy is that it would have cost little in the way of time or money for the healthcare providers to simply have communicated important information and updates to one another. It is a simple and effective plaintiff's theme.

Failure to Fully Inform Patients

Similar approaches have been promoted for issues of informed consent. For example, using a chart titled "The Meeting That Didn't Happen" allows a plaintiff's attorney to list all of the things the doctor should have told the patient about risks, benefits, alternatives, and post-treatment expectations, but failed to explain to the patient. This is particularly effective when the patient contends that had she been completely informed, she would have refused the treatment or surgery.

Current cultural expectations for increased information regarding medical and health issues on the part of patients renders this argument particularly effective. In fact, some state statutes now refer to "shared decision-making" models that reflect an increased expectation for patient involvement. The assumption is that patients not only need but also demand a maximum amount of information in order to participate fully in decision-making about their care. No patient or family member of a patient wants to feel they have been left in the dark by their healthcare providers. Many practices even have established "portals" that give patients access to their medical records and test results, and through which they can interact and communicate with their healthcare providers. This is expected to be a growing trend.

The Patient "Fell Through the Cracks"

Hospitals, clinics and doctor's offices are busy places. Thousands of patients are evaluated, diagnosed and treated every year. In that process, charts can get misplaced, notes can be misfiled, and communications can be less than ideal. From this reality has grown a popular plaintiff's theme that resonates loudly with jurors: the patient was treated with such indifference that he or she simply "fell through the cracks" of the hospital or practice, and failed to receive needed care or treatment. Evidence of this misfortune is reinforced through questioning during which the defendant doctor or nurse confesses that necessary care was not ordered, medication was not given, or nothing can be recalled about the patient or her care.

Given that a lawsuit may materialize years after the treatment in question, it is not unusual for a healthcare provider to have little if any memory of a specific patient. However, no patient wants to believe they were merely a number and that their physician has no recollection of them as a person, especially if there was a complication or unfortunate outcome. Plaintiff attorneys often argue, "The doctor has no memory of the patient or the treatment she provided. The only thing the doctor has is her chart." If not countered, plaintiff's counsel can score a direct hit with this theme.

Putting Profit Before People

In certain kinds of cases, opposing counsel may attempt to plant the idea that the organization's or the doctor's decisions regarding the care of the patient was motivated more by profit than by genuine concern for the patient's welfare. Questions about the doctor's position in a practice, how he is paid, bonus incentives, and productivity quotas derive from this theory. The suggestion that the more patients a doctor sees each day, or the more surgeries she performs, the more money she makes can be a compelling argument for jurors who feel their own time with physicians is limited.

Doctors who boast about the volume of patients seen or the number of procedures performed each day, and nurses who complain about high nurse-patient ratios, can unknowingly play into this plaintiff theory. Statistics that may be intended to impress opposing counsel or induce sympathy for one's workload will likely be used to argue the healthcare provider was over-worked, inattentive, or greedy. This strategy can incite anger among jurors and a desire to punish the defendant with a large plaintiff's verdict to offset any ill-motivated monetary gains or profit-driven policies.

EFFECTIVE RESPONSES TO PLAINTIFF'S THEMES

Every physician being deposed or being questioned at trial will be faced with questions at some point regarding patient safety, the standard of care, omissions in the medical record, and other areas related to common plaintiff theories. Here are some suggested counter-themes that, when woven strategically into the defense, can effectively offset powerful plaintiff themes and provide a basis for answering challenging questions that flow from plaintiff theories.

Differential Diagnosis is a Process, Not a Checklist

The requirement that you eliminate any imminently life-threatening conditions with which a patient presents can be an over-simplification that stems from misunderstanding the process of developing and using a differential diagnosis. On this issue, it may be necessary to clarify the process for plaintiff attorneys.

Be clear in your answers to such questions that the differential diagnostic process is not one of elimination so much as a process of determining probability of a specific condition. The differential can change over time as more information is accumulated. It uses symptoms certainly, but it also relies on the patient's medical history, your medical knowledge and experience, test results, the physical examination, and discussions with the patient. While risk of death is a critical factor, a physician also has to consider what is reasonable, logical, probable, and consistent with presenting symptoms. An old adage applies: "When you hear hoof beats, you think first of horses, not zebras."

> Q: *What did you do to rule out heart attack when Mr. Doe came to the ER complaining of chest pains?*
>
> A: *I took a medical history and discussed his recent activity, performed a thorough physical exam, ordered and then read his EKG as normal, and treated him prophylactically by giving aspirin.*

Some Medical Treatments Involve Risk

For decades, the rally cry of plaintiff attorneys has often been "We've been wronged and the jury must right the wrong." The primitive brain strategy proposed in *Reptile* has created a new flag around which plaintiff attorneys can rally: "Not just my client, but *you* must be protected from the dangers inflicted by negligent doctors." The notion that the greater the danger, the more the reptile (i.e., the juror) cares can be persuasive. Appealing to people's innate need for safety has considerable juror appeal.

No healthcare provider would deny that patient safety is critical. But while plaintiff attorneys may attempt to persuade jurors that physicians can and should guarantee the safety of their patients, healthcare providers know it is impossible to completely avoid or prevent risks when treating patients. In reality, there are situations in which patients must be put at risk in order to treat them successfully. Chemotherapy for the treatment of cancer is inherently risky—it is, after all, a form of poison. Surgery to remove a tumor or repair an abdominal injury carries certain inherent risks, but it is less dangerous than doing nothing. Angiograms, while essential to diagnose potential artery blockages, can be life-threatening. Some drugs can result in serious side effects, but without them the condition could worsen considerably. The alternative is to do nothing, which is perhaps a very unsafe direction to take.

Perhaps the most effective response to questions regarding patient safety is that in some cases, it is necessary to put patients at risk in order to treat them effectively. The best a physician can do is control risks or lessen the impact of a possible complication. Without denying the importance of patient safety, these realities need to be incorporated in effective answers. The following exchange represents one possible way to respond:

> Q: Doctor, wouldn't you agree with me that patient safety should be the guiding principle in diagnosing and treating patients?
>
> A: Ensuring patient safety is always at the forefront, and this is why patients are informed of the important or material risks and possible complications, and their consent to these risks is required before treatment can begin.

Each Patient and Each Situation is Unique

In some medical negligence lawsuits, plaintiff attorneys attempt to apply generalized rules, hospital protocols, and medical algorithms (step-by-step procedures) when asking jurors to decide whether the doctor has erred. There is little room in a plaintiff attorney's lexicon for "typically," "possibly," or "in most cases." From a plaintiff attorney's perspective, the argument is "When Dr. Smith observed condition X, he violated the standard of care by not doing Y." This sort of linear thinking could be disastrous to the practice of medicine.

In reality, there are many situations in which "it depends," or "in some cases but not all," or "it can vary from patient to patient" are more appropriate responses, given the specific patient's situation, condition, medical history, personal choices, or a variety of other factors that go into medical judgment and decision-making. It is important to resist any attempt to elicit agreement with a generalized statement regarding medical care and treatment that does not apply to the specific patient being discussed.

What Was Known at the Time

It is very difficult for attorneys, physicians, and jurors, to overcome hindsight bias when judging a poor medical outcome. Perfect medicine and completely accurate decisions are easy to evaluate after-the-fact: "If only the doctor had ordered an MRI," or "The doctor should have known the ureter had been transected." But the question jurors must be educated to understand is not whether better care *could* have been delivered; the issue is whether reasonable care was given, based on what was known or believed at the time. *Couldn't* you have ordered an MRI? Perhaps. *Shouldn't* you have gone immediately to the hospital when the patient's oxygenation level dropped below 85%? Perhaps. *Mustn't* you telephone a patient when an important appointment is missed? Perhaps. However, the issue is not whether some action could have or should have been taken, but whether you had solid reasons at the time to have taken that action or not, based on information available at the time and your best clinical judgment.

In responding to questions such as these, it is important for you to recall all of the treatment options that were being considered at the time, not just the obvious choice decided in hindsight. Making a list of the various pieces of information that were being processed over the course of the patient's treatment clarifies the options being considered at the time. Being prepared with specific reasons why an MRI was not ordered or why an X-ray was not taken, for example, will enable you to respond to hindsight questions with more confidence rather than second-guessing your decision. To be effective, your answers must help jurors see the logic of the decision-making at the time, not the intuitive "should have" reaction that is often the basis for malpractice claims.

It's More Complicated Than That

Many people prefer low effort thinking—it's black or white, right or wrong, appropriate or misguided. Plaintiff themes such as "It was obvious!" and "How could the doctor have missed something so simple?" have innate appeal because they are clear and easy to understand. The defense's themes are often more complicated: "There are many factors to consider." or "The patient had a complicated medical history that had to be taken into account." This requires defendant physicians to construct their own safety rule, such as in the following examples of effective responses:

> A: *I did the best I could under the circumstances, using my best clinical judgment at the time.*
>
> A: *Ms. Doe was made aware of the risks and she chose to have the procedure.*
>
> A: *The therapy resulted in a significant complication, but her life was saved by the treatment because she would have otherwise died within six months.*

For jurors to understand the principle you followed, they must be able to follow your thinking—what information you were weighing, what factors you were considering, or what your past experience dictated. It will be up to you to explain the logic and progression of your decisions in terms the average person can assimilate. The ability to make the complex understandable, and to enable jurors to imagine themselves in your situation at the time, is the hallmark of an effective healthcare witness.

The Standard of Care Does Not Mean Perfect Care

It is surprising how often doctors can be maneuvered into agreeing they violated the standard of care. Here is an example of how a doctor could be led down the path of admitting she had been negligent:

> Q: *Doctor, you would agree with me that a simple X-ray is the gold standard, or the standard of care, when it comes to a puncture wound in which foreign matter may be lodged, right?*
>
> A: *Yes, I would have to agree.*
>
> Q: *So if a doctor failed to order an X-ray when a patient came into the ER with a puncture wound sustained by stepping on a piece of metal while wearing flip-flops, that would be a violation of the standard of care, wouldn't it?*
>
> A: *I'd have to agree.*
>
> Q: *You didn't order an X-ray when Ms. Doe came into the ER did you?*
>
> A: *No, I did not. I explored the wound and found no foreign matter.*
>
> Q: *But a later X-ray of her seriously infected foot revealed foreign matter, didn't it?*
>
> A: *Yes.*
>
> Q: *So your failure to order a simple X-ray was a violation of the standard of care, right?*
>
> A: *I guess I would have to agree with you.*

By getting agreement that an X-ray was the standard of care, the doctor was trapped into admitting that if she did not order an X-ray, she violated that standard. In essence, she admitted liability. Let's look at where it all went wrong.

The legal definition of the standard of care is what a *reasonable* healthcare provider would do under similar circumstances. It is not perfect or ideal care, nor is it care that can only be provided in certain locales. It is the kind of care that falls under the large middle portion of the bell curve—average care, reasonable care, ordinary care. Attempts to persuade you that your care fell below what is in actuality an ideal standard must be resisted. When asked if your care indeed fell below standards, the most effective response is almost always, "Given what I knew at the time, my care was reasonable under the circumstances." Be prepared to identify what those circumstances were.

Confusing Guidelines and Standards

Plaintiff attorneys often confuse practice guidelines, hospital policies, treatment protocols, and utilization review procedures with the standard of care. They are not. For example, hospitals may refer to documentation policies as "standards of care" but this is different from the legal definition. Risk management or safety departments in clinics and hospitals may have policies with regard to patient safety, but these are not likely standards of care as defined in the law. Rather, they are most often formulated to be used in conjunction with sound clinical judgment. Always resist being forced to concede that practice guidelines and hospital policies represent standards of care for medical professionals.

Highway Rules Are for Highways, Not Medicine

Medicine is not practiced by rules or road signs; it is not a cookbook of techniques and procedures that can be followed by anyone who can read. It is carried out according to current practice guidelines, comprehensive training, timely research, hospital policies, clinical judgment based on experience, the unique aspects of a patient and his medical history, available resources, and many other factors. The standard of care is not a booklet of concrete rules to be followed rigidly. While plaintiff attorneys would like to draw the analogy between driving skill and medicine, it is a comparison that simply doesn't apply. Be cautious about questions that incorporate labels such as "rules," "policies," and "gold standards." Your "rule" is to reject the simplistic premise that medicine can be reduced to such elementary principles.

Medical Personnel Frequently Communicate

"Failure to communicate" and "communication breakdown" are simple, easily understood themes often used by plaintiff's counsel to suggest that the lack of proper or sufficient exchange of information about a patient led to a tragic outcome. While it can be challenging to communicate with other caregivers in busy settings, involving dozens of personnel working in different shifts, it is critical to remember that communication is a fundamental part of the medical professional's role. Remember also that how medical professionals communicate with each other is different from how they communicate with patients.

There are many ways in which doctors and nurses communicate among and between each other. It is important to clarify that any and all of the following forms of communication are consistently relied upon in a medical setting:

1. **Medical records.** Here is where significant observations and changes in patient status are documented. While plaintiff attorneys are quick to point out information that is absent from the record, implying insufficient record-keeping, the practice is to chart "by exception." If a piece of information is not in the record, it most likely means there was no change in the patient's status or it was not pertinent to the patient's care. The argument that "if it is not in the record, it did not occur" is an absurd one. It would be impossible to document everything about a patient's care; to do so would leave little time for patient care.

    It may also be appropriate to acknowledge that while medical records are important, they do contain errors, as it would be nearly impossible to edit them, identify inaccuracies, and make corrections. Since medical records are not like other documents that are proof-read and corrected to make certain they are perfect, it would be unreasonable to have such an expectation. Caregivers strive to be as accurate as possible, but in reality errors sometimes occur.

2. **Patient rounds.** One of the main purposes of making rounds on patients is for the providers to exchange information not only with each other, but also with patients.

3. **Shift changes and call hand-off.** Whenever a different doctor or nurse assumes responsibility for the care of a patient due to shift changes or changes in the professional who is on call, there is exchange of information in status conferences or hand-off communications. These are not usually documented, but can be verified because they are professional practices or routines that rarely if ever vary.

4. Patient contacts. When medical personnel are together in the patient's room, there is always opportunity for patients to inquire about their status, ask questions, provide information needed by caregivers, and communicate concerns. While taking vital signs, nurses often mentally note the patient's level of arousal, skin color, behaviors indicative of pain, and many other important signs of patient status. These exchanges and observations are so embedded in patient care practices that doctors and nurses often forget how frequently such observations and communications actually occur.

Whenever plaintiff's counsel suggests a lack of communication was a key factor in a patient's unfortunate outcome, it is important to recall the many non-documented settings in which important communication occurs on a routine basis.

Recollections of Patients

Asking a doctor what he recalls about a patient (without reference to the chart) can be interpreted as a request to recite physical characteristics, specific details of treatment, or a litany of memories about the patient's progression of treatment. Not so. All that may be required to extinguish the implication of indifference is to reference, for example, the patient's initial situation: "I recall that she was in considerable back pain when she came to see me." Or you might comment on the patient's outcome: "I recall that she was anxious to have the testing done as soon as possible, and she had a bad reaction to the dye used." Or you may recall a fact related to a patient's wishes: "I recall that he did not want a colostomy under any circumstances."

It is not uncommon for a plaintiff's attorney to challenge your recollection of a patient by arguing you have "no memory of the patient or the treatment provided other than the medical chart." The intention is to make you appear uncaring, thoughtless, or dismissive of your patients, but such assertions are rarely true. In addition to what was charted, you have training, experience, and professional routines to rely on and you should not hesitate to say so.

When the patient encounter is very brief and quite a few years in the past, as is often the case when the patient was in the Emergency Department only briefly or had only one office visit with the doctor, it is understandable that the doctor or nurse may not recall much if anything about the patient. In such situations, it is often best to simply explain the lack of recall: "Unfortunately I have no present recollection about Ms. Doe, as my care and examination were directed toward her need to be admitted. I was focused more on ensuring she received care than on what she looked like."

COMBATING PLAINTIFF THEORIES CAN BE CHALLENGING

To be successful, plaintiff attorneys must convince jurors that the practice of medicine is clear-cut—a black-and-white set of rules to which healthcare providers must adhere, specific steps that must be taken, or concrete checklists that must be followed when treating patients. Plaintiff's counsel must appeal to a juror's sense of indignation, using hindsight analysis and appealing to beliefs and expectations that perfect care is everyone's right. As a defendant it will be up to you and your attorney to educate jurors about the complexity of medicine and enable jurors to "stand in your shoes" as decisions were made and actions taken.

One of the strongest defenses you have to emotional appeals is to focus on the facts: what you did and why you did it in order to provide good care. Focus on information known at the time and avoid second-guessing or hindsight analysis of your actions and decisions. Remember that it is information, balanced by clinical judgment and concern for patient safety that drives medical decisions. Although jurors often feel sympathy for plaintiffs, they are usually critical of lawsuits based largely on emotional appeal and are most often guided in their decisions by verifiable facts.

10

LITIGATION AND ELECTRONIC MEDICAL RECORDS (EMRs)

> *This special chapter, written by Bertha Fitzer, J.D., is intended to alert defendant doctors about issues that can arise in a deposition or at trial with regard to Electronic Medical Records (EMRs)*

Electronic Medical Records are designed to improve communication between members of the healthcare team, and between patients and their physicians. However, the transition to EMRs carries with it some serious challenges for a healthcare provider who is being sued, and the attorney preparing his or her defense. Using EMRs in a lawsuit, for example, can provide plaintiff attorneys an opportunity to portray a doctor as incompetent, careless, disorganized, or dishonest. With the advent of EMRs have also come heightened expectations about what a doctor should know about a patient's medical history. In addition, the way in which data are entered into EMRs can lead to unintended errors or omissions. For some defense attorneys, the transition from paper to electronic record-keeping has complicated the task of obtaining and using records necessary to defend a doctor's care.

CHANGING PATIENT AND JUROR EXPECTATIONS

Unquestionably we live in an age of instant and frequent communications. Your patients and the jurors who will evaluate your legal case are accustomed to, and have learned to expect pertinent and comprehensive information in a much more timely fashion than in the past decades. Along with the development of electronic medical records has come patient access to their personal records on line through "My Chart" or similar interactive communication links. On-line charts are used to communicate test results to patients, schedule appointments, and provide an avenue for patients to request additional information or express concerns about their treatment.

One side effect of this trend is that now when patients review test results and reports on-line, they are more likely to use internet access to research the implications of test findings, and this can give rise to both fears and/or heightened expectations.

The emergence of EMRs is also affecting juror expectations regarding medical record-keeping. Jurors now expect that electronic records ensure greater access to data between providers and/or historical data such as information regarding a patient's earlier treatments and prior hospital admissions. These heightened expectations bring with them specific challenges to attorneys who will be defending your care.

CLAIMS OF SPOLIATION AND THE DANGERS OF SCREEN SHOTS AND PULL DOWN MENUS

One of the first events in your lawsuit will be a request through your attorney for the patient's complete medical records. Experienced attorneys will request not only the actual records, but also any data embedded in the software. Be wary of these requests and prepare documents as thorough as possible in responding to them. The plaintiff's attorney may be setting up your defense for what is called a "spoliation" claim. This is essentially a claim that you or your attorney did not properly answer the discovery requests, or that a document was hidden, altered, or destroyed so as to render it unusable as evidence. Whether the claim is that you destroyed evidence or simply failed to produce relevant records, the legal result is the same: the Court can impose significant fines, exclude your evidence, or issue a ruling that the jurors can consider such deficits as evidence of your liability.

To preclude a spoliation claim, it is a good idea to review relevant software programs with your attorney, your office manager, and/or the facility IT person if it appears opposing counsel is seeking information embedded in the software. Examples of these include pull down menus that recommend additional tests or courses of action if a specific finding is made. The additional time required to conduct such a search is outweighed by the potentially devastating effect of a Court ruling that will impede your defense.

EXPLAINING AUTO POPULATE ENTRIES

Once you have provided the patient's complete record to your attorney, the next challenge will be to answer questions about the record during your deposition and/or at trial. A troublesome feature of electronic medical records is the auto populate feature which allows incorrect or outdated patient data to persist in the records despite your office's best efforts to ensure accurate entries. Be prepared to identify those portions of the records which appear to be created through the auto populate feature. You also must be prepared to explain how errors that may appear in the records did or did not impact your care.

The auto populate feature has also increased exponentially the sheer volume of medical records, making the process of locating pertinent information within the records difficult. Your attorney's office can assist by organizing and summarizing medical records before your deposition. Your attorney should make certain that each page of the records you have produced is electronically numbered. Voluminous records, such as extended hospital stays, should be put in a medical chronology with dates for key events coordinated with the sequential page numbers. Organizing in this fashion early in the litigation process allows you, your attorney, and any experts supporting your care to "be on the same page" when reviewing and analyzing your care.

UNREALISTIC COMMUNICATION EXPECTATIONS

In medical school you may have been taught that if it isn't in the chart, it didn't happen. This adage was meant to reinforce the need to chart all critical and relevant information regarding patient care. Electronic medical records have created a new challenge. You will now be expected to know the complete medical record, including information from distant prior hospitalizations and data contained in the charts of other providers linked to you by access to the same EMRs. The simple response that you did not see the records will make you appear unprofessional and uncaring.

Both your attorney and the jury will need to understand which records are routinely consulted in treating a patient at various stages of his or her care. Issues as to when certain medical records become available may also be important. Finally, be prepared to explain that while it is crucial to be aware of certain data in the medical record, the primary exchange of pertinent information is between you and your patient. Be prepared to defend your care based on the clinical presentation and the symptoms the patient shared with you at the time of your treatment encounter.

IMPORTANCE OF MEDICAL RECORDS TO JURORS

Jurors rely heavily on medical records because they are often considered more objective than testimony given by witnesses on either side. That is, the plaintiff may exaggerate, relay only selective memories, or fail to disclose important facts; the defendant doctor can be seen as putting his or her "spin" on the facts and events in the case. But written records are viewed as the most independent sources of information, and for that reason, are often heavily relied upon by jurors. They often find and note minor errors in a patient's medical record (e.g., wrong age, incorrect weight, etc.) that are given more weight than anticipated because they can be viewed as evidence of inattention, hurried record keeping, and carelessness.

Addressing Inconsistencies in the Medical Records

When pointed out by a plaintiff's attorney, inconsistencies in the record can give the appearance that you are untruthful. You can head off this ambush by making certain you are aware of the inconsistencies before the deposition takes place. Being prepared to address and explain the inconsistencies will take some of the potential sting out of plaintiff's questions.

After identifying any inconsistencies, examine your processes to determine how and why they occurred. Was it due to the auto populate process? Which version of the record is correct and why? What role, if any, did the incorrect information play in your treatment of the patient? Be ready to answer questions not only about the existence of the error or inconsistency, but its significance in the overall treatment of the patient.

Cryptic Entries, Errors, and Other Minor Faults

Not everything that is communicated between healthcare professionals, and between providers and patients, is in the medical record. Patient care would suffer if providers were required to keep such extensive records. By necessity, medical records are the vehicle for communicating pertinent patient information, often in shorthand fashion, between care providers, not as a vehicle to educate attorneys bringing lawsuits. In fact, medicine is known for its numerous shorthand notations, abbreviations, and acronyms that allow a great deal of information to be communicated efficiently. For example, a few letters in the chart can represent a rather lengthy discussion of risks, benefits, and alternatives to a treatment being considered; an acronym can convey an ingestion allowance for a pre-op patient or the frequency with which medications are to be dispensed.

Avoid apologizing for brief medical record entries. They are after all but snapshots of much longer and more complex series of events. If an important omission is noted by opposing counsel, there is no need to find excuses. You should admit there was an omission and either point out that the omission did not affect your care, or that the failure to document it does not mean it was not done. Some critical events do not warrant documentation because they are so routine (e.g., scrubbing, gloving and gowning before a surgery; changing gloves between patients, providing a non-prescription medication such as aspirin).

Errors in charting do happen. When an error in your charting is pointed out during a deposition or at trial, you must first make certain it is an actual error and not simply a misunderstanding or transcription typo. When it is truly an error, it is important to point out whether the error made any difference in your care. If it did make a difference, take responsibility for the outcome.

11

IF YOU GO TO TRIAL

*"There are two sides to every story.
And then there's the truth."*

—COURT TV

If your case does not settle, a trial date will be set for presenting it to a jury. In this chapter you will learn what happens at trial, how giving testimony at trial differs from deposition testimony, and how you should conduct yourself in the courtroom. By the time your case gets to trial, you will already have been deposed. In fact, many of the key witnesses at trial—plaintiff, experts, and other defendants, if there are any—likely have been deposed also. There will be few evidentiary surprises. The plaintiff's attorney already will have exposed you to cross-examination, assuming he is the same attorney who conducted your deposition. As a result, you will be more knowledgeable about plaintiff's claims and theories. Regardless of the experience you have had with depositions, however, giving testimony in front of a jury is a uniquely stressful event. This chapter will teach you how to be as effective at trial as you were in your deposition.

WHAT HAPPENS AT A TRIAL

At trial, motions are heard, a jury is selected and seated, opening statements are given, and opposing counsel then presents the plaintiff's case. Your defense will not be presented until the plaintiff's attorney has presented all of her witnesses and evidence. In most cases, you will not take the stand until the plaintiff has completed her entire case; then it is the defense's turn.

Your attorney's defense strategy dictates the order in which various witnesses are called to the stand, so you may not be called first. When you are called, your attorney will guide you through a series of questions to enable you to tell your version of events. This is called *direct examination*. When your attorney is finished, opposing counsel will *cross-examine* you. Then your attorney may want to clarify some of your answers or provide a fuller explanation to the jurors of some point raised in your cross-examination. Your attorney is allowed *re-direct examination* of you, and if opposing counsel chooses to do so, she may follow re-direct questioning with *re-cross*. If you fear giving an incomplete answer, set those fears aside. Your attorney can return to any issue raised by opposing counsel in cross-examination, thus allowing you to explain more fully an earlier answer.

It's possible, even likely, that you could be called as a witness by opposing counsel while the plaintiff's case is being presented. This is called being an *adverse witness*. It makes your job more challenging because you must make a good first impression on the jury under the worst circumstances—when you are being questioned by the plaintiff's attorney. Jurors are sometimes confused by this strategy and may assume you are being called as a witness for the plaintiff's case because your actions so strongly support that side.

When each side has rested its case, opposing counsel and your attorney each give a *closing argument*. This summation typically reviews for the jurors:

a. the case issues,

b. the burden of proof that must be met by the plaintiffs,

c. key evidence and testimony,

d. statements about how the law applies, and

e. arguments in support of the plaintiff's claims or the defense's themes.

It is during closing arguments that most of the psychological or emotional appeals to jurors are made.

On a par with plaintiff's opening salvo, a closing argument can be painful for you. Your flaws, having been carefully dissected in court, once again are summarized—often with dramatic intensity. Your medical competence, your character, your professional judgment, and your credibility will be rebuked. And while you listen to this verbal thrashing, you must remain calm, cool, and collected. You must be able to endure this criticism and maintain your conviction that you did everything you could to help the patient. Contrary behavior will be viewed by jurors as the "flinch of the guilty."

Although they are difficult to make, the decisions required of a jury are straightforward. First, what was the doctor's *conduct*—what did the defendant do or fail to do that is at issue? Second, did that conduct fail to meet accepted medical standards—was there *negligence* by the defendant? Third, if negligence occurred, did the physician's conduct result in harm to the patient—did the doctor's behavior *cause* the harm? Lastly, if the defendant's conduct caused the harm, what amount of money compensates the patient for his or her pain, suffering and financial losses—what are the *damages*? Thus, the jury's ultimate charge is to determine *negligence, causation,* and *damages*. In lawsuits involving multiple defendants, the jury is asked to apportion fault among the defendants. The plaintiff may also be assigned some fault if the facts show the patient contributed to the harm in some way.

HOW TRIAL TESTIMONY DIFFERS FROM DEPOSITIONS

While many of the techniques discussed in this book apply equally to deposition or trial testimony, there are several key differences. It is important to understand these differences and what they mean in terms of your behavior.

At Deposition

Primarily *cross-examination* by the plaintiff's attorney.

Answer *only* the question asked, in a very succinct form.

Not the place to "tell your story."

Eye contact with the questioning attorney.

Your role is to answer questions.

Your attorney is there as an observer, to voice objections if necessary, and to ensure that a proper record is made.

No jury is present.

Questioning by opposing counsel can be very broad.

Objections by your attorney are noted for the record, but you will most likely have to answer all questions anyway.

The setting is rather informal.

At Trial

Direct examination by your attorney and *cross-examination* by opposing counsel.

Answer your attorney's questions *fully* under direct examination.

This is the time to "tell your complete story" to the jury.

Eye contact is with the attorney and the jurors.

Your role is to be an "educator" of the jurors, rather than a "defendant."

Your attorney presents your side of the story and actively persuades the jury to decide in your favor.

A jury is present and will decide the case.

Questions from attorneys must be directly relevant.

Objections by your attorney will be ruled on by the judge before questioning can proceed.

The setting is very formal.

ANSWERING QUESTIONS AT TRIAL

The same listening skills you learned in chapter six apply at trial. Many of the questioning techniques and traps discussed in chapters seven and eight will be used by opposing counsel. Most of the rules you learned about answering questions at depositions will also apply at trial, with a few exceptions. If you go to trial, be certain to review these chapters.

Become *very* familiar with your deposition transcript. Expect to be asked many of the same questions at trial. Expect to be confronted with any discrepancies between answers you gave at the deposition and those you give at trial.

There are several major differences between answering questions at a deposition versus at trial:

1. At trial, **your answers must be delivered to the *jurors*,** as much as possible. They are the only people in the courtroom who have a vote, and they are the ones you need to educate and convince. If you do not look at them from time to time, and give your answers to critical questions directly to the jury box, your credibility will be seriously damaged. Being able to look someone "right in the eye" is an ageless standard for truth-telling. Not every answer requires eye contact, but for key questions it will be essential. Avoid addressing only one or two jurors who appear friendly; spread your eye contact as you would when speaking to any group.

2. At trial, ***how you* deliver your answers takes on much more importance** than in a deposition. Jurors are influenced not only by what you say, but how you look when you are answering questions on the stand. Do you look nervous? Are you wringing your hands? Are you looking at your feet? Does your voice sound pompous? Are you angry and resentful? The impact of your answer is highly dependent upon non-verbal cues such as confidence, demeanor, posture, and volume. A relaxed posture, with feet on the ground and torso leaning slightly forward, reflects earnestness and gives the impression that you are listening intently to the questions and are serious about giving an honest and straightforward answer.

3. At trial, **the ability to *maintain your composure* throughout questioning** is especially important. Having previously given a deposition, you already know what opposing counsel is after. This will help ease your apprehension, and somewhat reduce the stress of cross-examination. Your ability to remain calm, cooperative and professional, regardless of how heated the questioning becomes, are significant factors in how jurors assess your competence as a physician.

4. At trial, ***avoid dramatic changes* in your demeanor** between direct and cross-examination. If you are polite and confident in answering your attorney's questions, but hostile under cross-examination, jurors will wonder which face is the "real" you. Your conduct during rigorous cross-examination enhances your credibility and strengthens your image as a doctor who remains calm under fire. You should not express anger, or blame the patient or the patient's family, nor should you direct negative sentiments toward other defendants. Remember, too, that people associate truthfulness with calmness, and they associate lying with anger. On the other hand, don't over-control your emotions to achieve a grim look or poker face. To jurors, you could appear distant or uncaring.

HOW YOU SHOULD APPEAR TO JURORS

Most jurors hold medical professionals in high regard. They also have high expectations for them, and hold a somewhat idealized picture of what a "good doctor" should look and act like. Although not every physician is expected to mirror the image of the idealized "television doctor," jurors do expect you to embody the "The Four Cs":

- **Conscientiousness**
- **Compassion**
- **Competence**
- **Confidence**

To the extent you clearly project these characteristics on the stand, there will be fewer inconsistencies for jurors to reconcile between their image of a "good doctor" and you. Remember also that likeability translates into credibility: We tend to believe people we like and admire, and to disbelieve people we dislike and find disagreeable or offensive. The introduction of evidence by attorneys and the testimony offered by witnesses does not determine the outcome of a trial. Jurors must *believe* the evidence and testimony presented to them. This is why your credibility is so important.

Your goals at trial are simple and straightforward: tell the truth, win the esteem of jurors as a *person* (not just as a doctor), listen carefully to each question and give a responsive answer, be professional and pay attention to your courtroom demeanor. It is these accomplishments, more so than professional credentials and reputation that lead jurors to believe your testimony. Keep in mind that jurors listen both viscerally (with their "gut") and cognitively (with their brain). If they view you negatively, they are not likely to listen to you either.

Strive to present yourself as the doctor that people in the room would want to have care for them. No matter how strained you may be feeling, it is important to project the "The Four Cs." Hostile glances, frowning, shouting, arguing, hand wringing, and bad temper only convey guilt. Never enter into a shouting match with opposing counsel or attempt to outsmart him. Arrogance is equally deadly; it is one of the most frequently cited reasons why jurors do not believe witnesses. In the courtroom it is best to appear serious but not excessively grim, confident but not arrogant, and calmly respectful and attentive.

It is critical to address your responses to the jurors as much as possible, regardless of who is asking the questions. Making this look smooth and natural is challenging, as you do not want to appear to jurors to be overly coached. Few things turn off jurors more quickly than a doctor defendant who looks at the attorney when being asked a question, but who then swivels around to look at the jurors when answering the question. If you appear to be watching a tennis match, jurors will likely question your sincerity.

Even though you may understand the importance of looking at jurors, and may even have practiced this awkward choreography, high levels of anxiety can interfere. Many witnesses do a good job of looking at jurors at the beginning of questioning, when it is foremost in their minds. But as time goes by, and fatigue and anxiety settle in, witnesses resort to focusing exclusively on the attorney. Because they understand the importance of eye contact as a factor jurors use to determine witness credibility, some plaintiff's attorneys will make every effort to distract your attention away from jurors, or make it difficult to maintain your orientation to the jury box. Recognize this tactic if it occurs and resist it.

When you enter the witness stand, try positioning your chair slightly toward the jury box. When your attention is distracted, your physical orientation will bring you back in focus with jurors. If asked why are you are directing so much attention to the jurors (and not to plaintiff's attorney), an honest response might be: "I want to make certain the jurors can hear and understand my answers."

THE IMPORTANCE OF PRE-TRIAL PREPARATION

Given the major differences between depositions and trials, it is wise to hold a question-answer rehearsal before the trial. This "dry-run" should include practicing not only anticipated cross-examination questions, but also direct examination questions from your attorney. Far too many witnesses have gone to trial without knowing what to expect regarding their own attorney's style, pace, and demeanor. The time to become comfortable with your attorney's style is not on the witness stand. Jurors expect a high level of rapport between parties and their attorneys. A pre-trial preparation session will allow you to practice a smooth exchange of questions and answers with your own attorney before you get on the stand.

A pre-trial preparation session can also provide you with the opportunity to practice delivering answers to the jurors. Looking at the attorney while a key question is being asked, but delivering an explanatory answer to the jurors, can be awkward. Usually, we maintain body orientation and eye contact with the person with whom we are having a conversation. In the courtroom, there are no "conversations" except with the jurors, and no need to tell your story to attorneys—they already know it.

ABOUT THE JURY

One of the first things done at trial is the seating of a jury. Potential jurors will be questioned by both sides to determine if they have any biases that could preclude fairness. Biased jurors are excused. Your attorney also has *peremptory challenges*, usually three, that she can use to excuse a juror for any reason, without having to reveal the reason. (Note: There are some exceptions to this.) Your attorney's goal is to seat jurors who can understand the issues and be absolutely fair to you. Remember that the court system does not allow an attorney to "pick" your jury. At best, counsel is allowed to eliminate those people who would clearly be biased against you. In this sense, jurors cannot be "selected" but are rather "de-selected."

The issues to be decided in your case are judged by ordinary citizens, not by your professional peers. This means the ordinary person must be able to understand you and to follow your decision-making process. When jurors deliberate, they:

- are motivated to try hard and do the right thing.
- often reason from their own medical experiences or those of friends and family.
- are moved by sympathy for plaintiffs and the plaintiffs' families.
- judge the honesty of witnesses not only by what they say, but how they say it.
- give great weight to written documents such as medical records.
- draw common analogies to everyday life (marriage, work, home ownership) in order to understand complex issues.
- often simplify the evidence so they can understand it.

- are curious about and interested in medicine, anatomy, and treatments, but are easily overwhelmed by technical information.
- do consider insurance coverage, even though it cannot be addressed at trial.
- do hold patients partly responsible for certain outcomes and do understand the concept of "contributory negligence" by patients.
- almost always consider the portion of any damage award that the plaintiff's attorney would receive, even though instructed not to do so.
- form an impression of you early in the trial that impacts their decisions.

Selection of a jury in a medical malpractice case is a challenging task, and one to which few attorneys look forward. Be prepared to assist your attorney in whatever way she determines is appropriate. At the very least, she will want your input regarding signs of juror bias you may have noted. Your attorney may also hire a trial consultant to assist with jury de-selection.

BE AN EDUCATOR, NOT A DEFENDANT

One of your chief goals as a witness is to educate jurors so they can make logical, informed decisions. Some trial observers believe that witnesses who have the greatest impact on jurors are those who foster understanding by being good teachers. Jurors also give the greatest weight to evidence they can easily comprehend, and tend to recall it more consistently in deliberations. It is not uncommon in jury debriefings to hear jurors report, "We gave a lot of weight to Dr. Doe's testimony because he explained things in a way we could understand. Everyone else talked in mumbo-jumbo." or similar sentiments.

Teaching lay people about anatomy, treatments, surgical procedures, drug effects and complex aspects of medicine is a challenging task. Some of this work will be done by experts who have been hired, at least partly, for their ability to educate others. But never underestimate the importance of your role as an "expert" in patient care. You must tell jurors what you did and why you did it, in everyday language. You must clarify why you made certain decisions rather than others. You must describe in careful detail exactly what you did. A procedure you consider routine may require a very detailed, step-by-step or moment-by-moment description. Such painstaking and detailed explanations may be absolutely essential for jurors to comprehend the issues in the case. Don't expect jurors to simply "take your word for it" because you are the highly educated medical professional. They require complete answers and understandable reasoning regarding your care, regardless of your credentials and experience.

Keep in mind that jurors are silent listeners who cannot ask questions for clarification while you are speaking. You must anticipate what they may have difficulty understanding, and explain it methodically in everyday language. Use analogies, relate the information to common experiences, and confine your explanations to only what jurors need to know. Most doctors feel much more comfortable in the role of teacher, talking about familiar subjects, than they will ever feel as a "defendant." Above all, take your time. Trial is the time to tell your story, so make certain you tell your portion thoroughly, patiently, and honestly.

DEVELOPING RAPPORT WITH JURORS

The more distant people feel from you, or the less they feel they have in common with you, the easier it is for them to judge you harshly. If you are viewed by jurors as rich, cold, arrogant, uncaring, or incompetent, it will be easier for them to conclude that you are also a negligent doctor. On the other hand, people tend to be more forgiving of those they like. As a physician, there may exist a social and income gap between you and most jurors. It is up to you to close that gap, to "win their hearts and minds," and to present yourself first and foremost as a competent and conscientious person. Remember that the object is to win the respect of jurors as a *person*, not necessarily as a medical genius, so keep your language simple.

Building rapport with jurors requires the same skills you apply every day with patients. In order to gain a patient's trust and confidence, you must demonstrate good listening skills, explain things carefully in language she can understand, and anticipate her questions. It is no different with jurors. If you think of jurors as patients, and think of yourself as an educator who is informing your "patients," you will feel less intimidated in the courtroom.

When you take the witness stand, acknowledge the jurors with a smile and nod of your head. Then remember to orient your chair slightly toward them. This will make it easier to direct your answers to them without having to turn your head in an uncomfortable angle or bounce back and forth between counsel and jurors as though watching a tennis match. Imagine that you have a large audience that includes the jurors and the questioning attorney. You need not acknowledge the judge or direct any eye contact toward him or her unless the judge is asking you a direct question.

Other rapport building techniques include:

- **Look pleasant rather than grim.** Avoid the frightened look of a "deer in the headlights." Don't be afraid to smile when it's appropriate to do so.

- **Keep your volume high.** Some jurors may have trouble hearing if you speak softly. Speaking up also demonstrates you are sensitive to the acoustics and the jury's need to hear clearly. Volume is also associated with confidence.

- **Lean into** the jurors slightly when giving a longer explanation; appear to be including them in your story.

- **Become a teacher and a storyteller.** Animate your responses with variations in voice pitch and tempo. Answering questions in a bland monotone is boring and jurors may simply stop listening (or even fall asleep!).

- **Use your hands** and use visuals whenever possible. A picture is worth a thousand words, and jurors recall best what they have not only heard but also seen. Use models, pictures, summary charts, and any other visuals. At the very least, use your hands to show how large something was, where in the chest the incision was made, where the pancreas is located, and so forth.

- **Avoid treating the jurors as aliens.** They are not. They are neither witless nor heartless. Be yourself—the way you are with patients. Let jurors see the real doctor as you function every day, not the doctor who is being sued.

WHEN JURORS CAN ASK QUESTIONS

In many states, jurors are allowed to ask questions of any witness on the stand. Typically, this option can be exercised when both sides have completed their questioning of the witness. The judge then asks if there are any questions from the jurors. If so, the questions must be submitted in writing without identification of the juror posing the inquiry. After discussing the question with attorneys for both sides, a determination is made about the admissibility of the question. If it is an appropriate and admissible question, the judge poses the question to the witness, who is then expected to answer.

If you receive a question from the judge that has been posed by a juror, it is appropriate to look to the judge when the question is being read, and then turn to the jury to answer the question. Although you will not know which juror posed the question, you should assume that by looking at all the jurors when answering you are acknowledging your understanding that the question originated with someone in the jury box. Take questions posed by jurors very seriously—they do.

HEARING EXPERT WITNESS TESTIMONY

Expert witnesses for both sides play a large role at malpractice trials. In some venues, experts are mandatory for the plaintiff to establish a case, and for the defense to establish support for the care provided by the defendant. In venues where it is allowed, the experts will have been deposed and their opinions are known to both sides. Plaintiff experts who testify about the relevant standards of medical care can point out how and why they believe you deviated from those standards in your statements or actions. Their opinions regarding the causal link between the alleged negligence and the plaintiff's damages will be sought.

Other experts, such as rehabilitation professionals, economists, and long-term care providers may testify regarding financial losses, future needs and non-economic damages such as pain and suffering. Their role is to establish the parameters for damages. Expert witnesses hired by your attorney may also testify at trial on your behalf to counter the plaintiff's assertions in these areas.

Trials involving malpractice are sometimes referred to as cases of "dueling experts" because the debate of opposing expert opinions is a hallmark. The strength of expert opinions, and the ability of medical experts to persuade jurors with compelling testimony is critical. This is why experienced attorneys select and prepare expert witnesses carefully. Many malpractice attorneys admit that cases have been won or lost on the strength of expert testimony. As with all witnesses, the effectiveness of expert testimony is highly dependent upon good communication skills. A chief complaint of jurors is that medical experts often speak in technical jargon and "talk over the heads" of jurors.

Even though it is difficult to remain composed in a courtroom while a parade of plaintiff's experts (none of whom treated the patient) criticize your care and second-guess your judgment, this is exactly what you must do. Expressing your disagreement by violent head-shaking, rolling your eyes toward the ceiling, frantic note-writing to your attorney, and slapping the table will win no votes with jurors. Such behaviors are seen as disrespectful.

Whenever a witness is on the stand, give him or her your full attention, make notes of any testimony you may wish to discuss with your attorney, and maintain a calm demeanor. What would jurors conclude about the care provided by a defendant physician who lacks emotional control, is rude, impatient, or inattentive? It is best to regard plaintiff's medical experts simply as professionals with whom you disagree.

THOSE ANNOYING LITTLE HABITS

Perhaps with the exception of television news anchors, we all have mannerisms that have become such a part of our communication style we are no longer aware of them. What is tolerated or even joked about by colleagues or family may be serious annoyances for jurors. Try to control physical or verbal compulsions such as:

- finger steepling
- eyeglasses off and on
- ring twisting
- facial grimacing
- frowning
- hands in front of mouth
- mustache twirling
- hair twirling
- ceiling gazing

- foot tapping
- lint picking
- head scratching
- nail biting
- frequent throat clearing
- finger jabbing in the air
- pencil tapping
- arm crossing

At a trial, these mannerisms will distract jurors and divert their attention from your message.

DEMEANOR AND DRESS

You are subject to scrutiny every minute you are in the courtroom, not just when you are in the witness chair. Jurors are watching you for subtle signs of your competence. People judge others on the basis of grooming, facial expressions, and body language. At all times, be aware of the messages you are sending non-verbally.

If you need to tell your attorney something, wait until a break, or write it on a piece of paper and slide it casually to him. Don't pull on your attorney's sleeve, whisper, or cup your hand to his ear. Be certain to turn off your beeper and cell phone while in the courtroom. Never chew gum or eat snacks. Note that typically only water is allowed in the courtroom.

Watch out for nervous gestures also while seated in the courtroom with your attorney. Foot jiggling, finger steepling, clenching and unclenching your fists, rocking in your chair, knuckle cracking, typing on a laptop, tapping a pencil and other nervous habits are distracting. Jurors consider these as signs of fear and guilt.

Do not display negative reactions to the testimony of a witness on the stand, particularly the plaintiff. Rolling your eyes in disbelief, shaking your head in disagreement, grimacing, sneering, scowling or tapping your fingers in impatience reflects badly on you. Your look should be one of serious interest. Even when you strongly disagree with the testimony or opinion being offered, show no negative emotion. It is considered unprofessional and disrespectful by the jurors.

Never appear distracted in the courtroom. Do not read a newspaper, sketch landscapes, doodle, or re-organize your briefcase. Do not count the tile in the ceiling or whisper incessantly with a member of the attorney's staff. A lawsuit is serious business and jurors expect you to take it seriously. Do not stare at the jurors—it makes them uncomfortable. However, don't be hesitant to look at them occasionally when you are not testifying.

Dress professionally for court. The day you are expected to be on the stand, dress your best. Men should wear a soft blue shirt. Blue is friendlier than white and does not magnify any tendency you may have to blush or redden when flustered. Men should also avoid two-tone shirts, and any clothing that projects a corporate image, such as a black suit or a three-piece suit. Women should wear a conservative suit or dress with a modest length skirt. Avoid wearing anything black, as this has a "funeral" association. Avoid frilly blouses, low-cut or silky garments, loud colors, tight garments, and clothing that does not look clean and pressed.

Wear sensible shoes; do not wear tennis shoes, clogs, sandals, Uggs, platform high heels, or cowboy boots (unless you are in Texas). Wear little jewelry—a ring and watch for men; a ring, watch and small earrings for women. Wear nothing very expensive looking, such as a Rolex watch, large diamond ring, or massive gold chain. Flaunting wealth can motivate jurors to relieve you of some of it.

Men should get a hair and beard (if worn) trim before trial. Women should have a conservative hairstyle. Women who have long hair should tie it back or use combs to keep it out of their faces. Make-up and nail polish should be understated. The courtroom is not the place to demonstrate your hip fashion sense.

Be cautious about what you say in the halls, on break, in the elevator, or in the restroom. Jurors can be anywhere you are and can overhear. Be particularly careful prior to the start of the trial, when you are unaware of which people in the building or in the parking lot may end up on your jury.

Discuss with your attorney whether it is appropriate for your spouse or life partner to attend the trial. While your spouse's or partner's support may be important to your well-being, you must weigh the potential disadvantages: the person will also be under scrutiny by jurors.

If your spouse or partner does attend trial, the same rules regarding respectful and conservative demeanor apply. He or she must not react visibly to any criticisms that will be leveled against you, or make non-verbal gestures such as eye-rolling or head shaking that would be inappropriate. There should also be no obvious physical contact, such as hand-holding or hugging, while jurors are present. Such behavior is viewed as a sympathy ploy.

WHEN THE CASE IS GIVEN TO THE JURY

When both sides have presented their case and closing arguments are completed, the judge will instruct the jurors on the law that applies in your case. (In some states, instructions may be given earlier.) The jurors are given a verdict form which lists the questions they are being asked to decide. The verdict form typically includes questions regarding informed consent, negligence, causation and damages. In the case of multiple defendants, there may be a question requiring apportionment of fault (if found). If relevant in the case, jurors may be asked to determine if the plaintiff/patient contributed to the injury. Both sides have had an opportunity to provide input regarding the specific jury instructions given and the wording of the questions on the verdict form. Jurors are also told how many of them must agree (i.e., ten of twelve; six of eight; unanimous, etc.) in order to deliver a verdict.

There is no way to predict how long a jury will deliberate. Some courtroom veterans believe the shorter the deliberation, the more likely a defense verdict will be delivered because damage awards typically involve prolonged debate. Others believe a short deliberation is a positive sign for plaintiffs. In reality, there is little relationship.

Unlike television dramas, all parties typically leave the courthouse while the jury is deliberating. The court will notify the parties when the jurors have signaled they have reached a verdict. When everyone is re-assembled, the judge will read the verdict. Your attorney will advise you about whether he wishes you to be present for the reading of the verdict.

PRE-TRIAL JITTERS

Nervousness before trial is expected. Your attorney expects it, jurors expect it, and you should expect it. Some nervousness is actually beneficial; it will keep you alert and attentive. Be aware of how your nervousness tends to manifest: Do you talk too much? Pace? Laugh inappropriately? Does caffeine or nicotine magnify it? Nervousness is acceptable, but nervous behaviors may be annoying. Ease your anxiety as much as possible by taking deep breaths and stretching your neck and back muscles. Avoid caffeine before taking the stand if it makes you jittery. Don't take any medication unless you have some history of knowing its effect on you.

Several weeks before trial, begin using imagery to help reduce anxiety associated with thoughts of being in court. Picture yourself getting up the morning you will be on the witness stand. Imagine the thoughts you will have as you drive to the courthouse. Visualize your attorney introducing you to the jurors. Imagine being asked a difficult question. Imagine looking at the plaintiff. Which scenes make you most anxious? Practice relaxing while you visualize these scenes over and over until they lose some of their visceral strength.

Desensitizing yourself to the surroundings that trigger anxiety can be very helpful. If possible, visit the courtroom you will be in (or any courtroom, for that matter). Sit in the witness chair. Close your eyes and imagine opposing counsel asking the first question. Practice looking at the jurors while giving explanatory answers. Do some relaxation exercises as you feel tension mounting. Sit in the juror chair closest to the witness stand, and in the chair farthest away. What view will these jurors have of you, or of any flip chart or visuals you may be using? How are the acoustics? Is there a microphone on the witness stand? If so, practice speaking without leaning into the microphone.

Positive affirmations and self-talk can also help reduce any anxiety you may have. For example, try some of the following affirmations when you feel tension rising:

"I'm relieved and happy to be here today because I can now tell my full story."

"I'm confident about what I have to say to the jurors today."

"I am not here to convince others of my innocence, for I have done nothing wrong."

"This is a challenge, but one I have prepared for and know I will do well at."

"I have met and overcome great challenges in my life, and I will overcome this one."

"Adversity does not build character, it reveals it. I will reveal mine today."

"I expect to be nervous, but my nervousness will not interfere with my desire to tell my story effectively."

"I am looking forward to teaching the jurors, just as I do my patients."

POST-TRIAL DECOMPRESSION

Regardless of the trial outcome, expect to experience strong emotions once the process is completed. Physical and/or emotional exhaustion, elation, disappointment, gratitude, relief, cynicism, devastation, or sheer happiness may overwhelm you. Some defendant doctors cope with the post-traumatic stress of the trial conclusion by "hitting the ground running"—throwing themselves into their work at a fierce pace. Others need a physical and emotional vacation—a time to re-group with family and regain a sense of normalcy. Even if you can arrange only a weekend, plan something special with family or friends.

Doctors have reported that regardless of the outcome, their lives are irreversibly altered by a malpractice suit. Many feel more vulnerable, some are more risk-averse, others alter the way they practice medicine, a few become better communicators and record-keepers, several pay more attention to patient communication, some are humbled. A few become cynical and embittered; a few leave medicine to go into teaching or research. This is not a book on therapy, but two pieces of advice are appropriate:

1. Don't make any major decisions for at least a month following your trial.

2. Don't hesitate to seek professional counseling if you are still pre-occupied with the case after a reasonable period of decompression.

You have been through a long, stressful process, and as you often counsel your patients: Time will be the best medicine.

12
THE POCKET GUIDE

Back in college when you lacked the time, or perhaps the motivation to read an entire book, there were always "Cliff Notes." These condensed, cut-to-the-chase summaries lopped hours if not days off an overcrowded schedule. The value of those compact briefings is not lost here. In this final chapter are the condensed points, suggestions, tips, and traps you won't want to forget.

THINGS TO REMEMBER ABOUT MALPRACTICE LAWSUITS

1. The key determination in any malpractice lawsuit is whether your care fell below the "standard of care" for your specialty. Jurors do not always understand this concept and may apply their own definitions.

2. The plaintiff must prove his case by a "preponderance of the evidence" and must use medical experts to do so.

3. Yours is a civil case to determine liability and damages, not guilt or punishment.

4. Lawsuits are filed against even the best doctors and have little to do with your track record.

5. Most malpractice lawsuits are dropped or settled before trial; many are won at trial.

6. Lawsuits are won through team defense efforts; you are an important team member whose active participation is critical to success.

THINGS TO REMEMBER ABOUT EMOTIONAL REACTIONS

1. Common reactions include: annoyance, diminished confidence, self-criticism, overanalysis, resentment, anger, fear, anxiety, worry about loss of control, disbelief and denial. You can expect to experience some of these.

2. Expect to be on an emotional roller-coaster to some extent.

3. Being proactive and cooperating in your defense will help you regain some sense of control.

4. Positive self-talk and imaging will help reduce anxiety and have a calming effect.

5. It is intelligent, not weak, to rely on family and friends for emotional support.

THINGS TO REMEMBER ABOUT DEPOSITIONS

1. Depositions are taken to assist the *opposing party* and are of no benefit to you. A deposition is not the place to tell your story. Don't try to persuade opposing counsel that plaintiff's case is weak.

2. Depositions result in a typed transcript that will be thoroughly scrutinized by opposing counsel in the hopes of discovering damaging admissions, inconsistencies, falsehoods, or other facts not previously known to him.

3. Depositions are not conversations and none of the principles of polite social conversation apply. Just the opposite is true: question and answer exchanges proceed with completely different rules.

4. Opposing counsel's goals are to cast a wide net to gather information, evaluate your strength as a witness, and test her case themes.

5. Preparation for a deposition with your attorney is essential to your performance and you should insist on it.

THINGS TO REMEMBER ABOUT YOUR GOALS AT DEPOSITION

1. Tell the truth and don't guess.

2. Listen actively and carefully to every word in every question.

3. Be succinct, accurate, and precise in your answers.

4. Take your time and don't try too hard.

5. Keep your cool no matter how much tempers heat up.

THINGS TO REMEMBER ABOUT LISTENING

1. Everyday listening is different from the kind of active listening required at a deposition or trial.

2. Barriers to active listening include "out-listening" (listening only long enough to surmise what is being said), "selective listening" (hearing only what you want to) and "challenge listening" (focusing on your anticipated response rather than to what is being said). These barriers can prevent you from properly diagnosing and responding to questions under cross-examination.

3. Active listening is your most powerful weapon against opposing counsel. It protects you from being intimidated or trapped.

4. By listening carefully you can avoid common mistakes, such as jumping ahead to questions you anticipate, answering too quickly, improving upon weak questions, or becoming distracted.

5. Use your diagnostic skills to determine what kind of question you are being asked and clarify any misunderstandings before answering. Ask for clarification if the question is leading, ambiguous, hypothetical, or intended to be provocative.

6. Listen for "mental alarms" such as inflammatory words, mis-characterizations or misstatements, embedded assumptions, negative words, absolutes, double negatives, or ambiguous phrases.

7. Practice active listening by visualizing spoken words, paraphrasing, and correcting social speech.

THINGS TO REMEMBER ABOUT ANSWERING QUESTIONS

1. The most common errors are volunteering information, failing to listen carefully, and losing emotional composure. Most errors result from lack of understanding of the purposes and goals of the deposition.

2. The most common fears are that one's testimony will be manipulated or that opposing counsel will badger a witness into saying something unintended.

3. Many doctors fear memory failures, but there is no need to be overly concerned about this. In addition to your unassisted recall, you can rely on memory refreshers, records and lab results, and your professional routines.

4. Certain areas of questioning can be expected to be covered at your deposition. Since it's taken during the "discovery" phase, expect a wide range of questions, some of which may appear to you irrelevant.

5. There are certain rules you should follow in giving a deposition. The most important are to tell the truth at all times, listen carefully to every word in every question, keep your answers brief, make certain you understand a question completely before answering, stay within your realm of expertise, use positive action words to talk about what you did and maintain a professional demeanor.

6. Because attorneys are professional questioners, they're skilled at maneuvering you into certain response modes. You can avoid these tricks and traps if you are aware of them. Some common traps are putting words in your mouth, inviting you to volunteer information, cutting short your answers, jumping from topic to topic, pointing out inconsistencies, asking the same question in different forms, focusing on failures and inducing guilt, exaggerating the importance of inconsequential facts, and catching you off guard by dropping "bombshells."

7. While giving testimony, avoid negative words, medical jargon, hesitant language, and deferential titles such as "sir" and "madam."

THINGS TO REMEMBER ABOUT GOING TO TRIAL

1. It is unlikely your case will go to trial, but you should always be prepared to do so.

2. Your testimony at trial will be different than at deposition because this is now the time to tell your story.

3. At trial, view your role as one of educator, not defendant.

4. You will be subjected to direct examination by your attorney and cross-examination by opposing counsel.

5. Listen intently, diagnose questions, seek clarification and answer questions carefully, regardless of who is asking them.

6. Jurors will be evaluating not only what you say, but how you say it. Your demeanor on the witness stand should reflect the four Cs: Competence, Compassion, Confidence and Conscientiousness. You must win the esteem and respect of jurors if you hope to persuade them with your testimony.

7. You are being assessed by jurors at all times, so watch those nervous tics and annoying habits. Always be completely professional in and around the courtroom.

8. Pre-trial jitters are expected and can be reduced by familiarizing yourself with the courtroom before the trial, using imagery and positive affirmations, and using relaxation techniques. Some period of "decompression" may be needed after the trial is completed.

ABOUT THE AUTHORS

Angela M. Dodge, Ph.D., is the founding partner of a litigation consulting practice based in the Seattle-Tacoma area of Washington State. An experienced trial consultant and social psychologist, she has helped hundreds of attorneys across the country with trial strategy, witness preparation, jury de-selection, pre-trial research, and post-trial juror interviews. She has assisted with cases in all areas of the United States, but has focused on Pacific Northwest venues.

Dr. Dodge specialized in working on medical malpractice defense cases, and she has prepared several thousand doctors, nurses, physician assistants and other care providers to give more effective and compelling testimony. In addition to her practice, she is the author or co-author of four other guidebooks for attorneys and witnesses. She is now retired from consulting work, but continues to manage the firm's publications.

In addition to her expertise in professional malpractice, Dr. Dodge provided consulting services on several thousand civil cases, including a number of high profile lawsuits. Her experience with witness preparation and trial strategy has been amplified through hundreds of post-verdict juror interviews.

Angela earned her undergraduate degree summa cum laude at the University of North Dakota (1972) and her doctorate at the University of South Carolina (1976). On a personal level, Angela is a devoted animal rescue and protection advocate.

Steven F. Fitzer, J.D. (Deceased) was a respected trial attorney and senior partner in the law firm of Fitzer, Fitzer, Veal & McAmis, P.S. in Tacoma, Washington. He passed away in August of 2019 and his firm continues the practice as Fitzer Veal Law P.S. in the same location.

In practice since 1976, Steve's specialty was medical and legal professional liability defense. Over the course of his private practice career, he worked with thousands of witnesses, including doctors, nurses, physician assistants, and other medical professionals. He was a Fellow in the American College of Trial Lawyers, and served as the Past Chair of the Litigation Section of the Washington State Bar Association. He was a member of the American Board of Trial Advocates, and participated in their Masters in Trial demonstrations. He also belonged to the Federation of Defense and Corporate Counsel, was a former Trustee of the Washington Defense Trial Lawyers association, and a member of the Defense Research Institute (DRI). Mr. Fitzer holds Emeritus membership in the Robert J. Bryan Puget Sound Inns of Court, and he was a frequent speaker at local and national seminars on legal and risk management issues.

In addition to collaborating on this publication, Mr. Fitzer is Chapter Author of the Washington Civil Procedure Deskbook (Second Edition, 2002) and a Section Author of the Washington Civil Trial and Evidence Manual (Fifth Edition, 2004). He was an avid fundraiser for Mary Bridge Children's Hospital. His wife, Bertha Fitzer, J.D., with whom he practiced, continues the law firm in Tacoma, Washington.

Steve received his bachelor's degree cum laude from Carroll College (1973) and his law degree from Marquette University (1976).

FOR CONSULTATION SERVICES, PRESENTATIONS,
OR EDUCATIONAL SEMINARS, CONTACT:

John H. Ryan, Ph.D.
Litigation Psychologist
(509) 998-9672
E-mail: jryan@dodgeconsulting.com

For additional copies or other
litigation-related publications, visit our website:

www.dodgepublications.com

ORDER ON THE WEBSITE AND RECEIVE
20% OFF ALL BOOKS
AND FREE MEDIA MAIL SHIPPING!

TO ORDER ADDITIONAL COPIES OF:

WHEN GOOD DOCTORS GET SUED

2nd EDITION

$34.95 USD
($27.96 if ordered on the website)

Contact:
Dodge Publications
(253) 857-7716

E-mail: info@dodgepublications.com

Website: www.dodgepublications.com